RELATIONAL

ACUITY 3.0

Cultivating Kingdom Relationships

Tiffany Buckner

Relational Acuity 3.0
Cultivating Kingdom Relationships

©2022, Tiffany Buckner
www.tiffanybuckner.com
info@tiffanybuckner.com

Published by Anointed Fire House

Edited by:
Anointed Fire House
J. Junga
Iman A.

ISBN: 978-1-955557-26-9

TABLE OF CONTENTS

INTRODUCTION

Relational Acuity 3.0 can best be described as a book of revelation! This information-rich guide is the perfect tool for people who desire to grow their relational acumen to degrees unimaginable; this is especially for individuals who believe that they are called to ascend the ranks in life, business, ministry and society. This is because relationships aren't just designed for entertainment; every relationship that we find ourselves a part of has a pulse and a purpose. Howbeit, most people waste their time in barren relationships simply because they are dealing with toxic loyalty, ungodly soul ties and the fear of starting over or being alone. Howbeit, this won't be your story; not anymore! Relational Acuity 3.0 is designed to give you the confirmation and the confidence you need to move forward so that you can and will fulfill your God-given assignment and enjoy the peace that Christ afforded you.

In this powerfully engaging book, you will come to understand why some of your relationships fell through the cracks, how to position the people in your life so that your relationships are both productive and beneficial, and how to understand when a relationship has expired. This book also touches on the topic of demonology! You will learn how unclean spirits weaponize soul ties with the sole intent of limiting your movement in the Earth. This is a book of healing, this is a book of power and this is a book of deliverance!

Relational Acuity 3.0 is more potent than it is practical, even though it is an easy read. Yes, this mind-boggling book is filled with wisdom, revelation and information that will help you to become more strategic and intentional whenever you begin to build new relationships, regardless of whether you're a babe in Christ or a seasoned believer. This book will also help you to properly categorize and rearrange your current relationships so that the blessings of God will flow without incident in your life!

THE SHAPE OF A SEASON

Every relationship has a purpose, whether that purpose is God-instituted, human-instituted or demonically driven. In truth, you'd be surprised at the percentage of relationships that are demonically arranged. Don't get me wrong. I'm not saying that one of the parties in any given relationship is an undercover agent for the devil. I am saying, however, that wherever there are voids, you will find demonic activity since voids are but empty spaces in the soul. These empty spaces are dark chambers or dark rooms, and in these rooms, there is a throne called the heart. Yes, every dimension of you has its own heart, and I'm not talking about a blood-pump. I'm talking about a seat or a core; this is where we get our core beliefs. It goes without saying that God should be sitting on the throne in each of these centers, but when we have not studied and shown ourselves approved, those spaces become or remain dark. Keep in mind that every dimension of us is a kingdom within itself, and Satan and his angels are citizens of the kingdom of darkness. They want to keep people ignorant because the absence of the Word sets the stage for their presence. And because it is human nature to need answers whenever we have questions, we oftentimes fill in the blanks with the answers that are most sensible or satisfying to us. This is what it means to lean to your own understanding, which is what God instructed us not to do in Proverbs 3:5. If we're honest, we can admit that most of our exes were nothing but void-fillers; they solved a problem, whether that problem was loneliness, rejection, a desire to feel wanted, financial distress, and the list goes on. The same is true for our friends. We've formed relationships, both knowingly and unwittingly, to pacify an issue that surfaced in our lives.

Every season has a shape. It has widths, heights and depths; it has levels, ranks and dimensions. And remember, a season is not just a space of time when the Heavens open or close; a season is a mindset. It is the space of time that you are locked in a dimension or a neighborhood of thinking; it represents the access to revelation and information that you have at any given period, and not just access to information, but the ability to chew or understand that information. This means that every season has its own teeth. This is why Apostle Paul rebuked the Corinthians in 1 Corinthians 3:2-3 with these words: "I have fed you with milk, and not with meat: for hitherto ye were not able to bear it, neither yet now are ye able. For ye are yet carnal: for whereas there is among you envying, and strife, and divisions, are ye not carnal, and walk as men?" Like any good leader, Apostle Paul had to recognize what the churches he covered could chew and understand, versus what they could not ruminate or digest, and it is clear to us, the readers, that their immaturity was somewhat disappointing to him. In other words, he saw the shape that the Corinthian church was in;

the same is true for every church that was under his leadership. Every letter that the apostle wrote to the churches he covered were not a newly instituted set of commandments designed to replace the Mosaic Law, as some religions would have you believe, but the goal of each letter was to whip each church into shape. This would allow them to fit into the seasons they had been granted access to, after all, every season comes with a measure of revelation; this revelation, when ruminated, is beneficial for the advancement of the church; it allows us to move forward in spiritual things. This means that we can be outside of a God-instituted season, all the while holding the keys to that season. Think of a season as a place, and whenever you are in the season that God has granted you access to, you are simultaneously in the will of God, but outside of that place, you will find a wilderness. While the wilderness is a season within itself, it is not your place of destiny. Consider the plight of the Israelites. They had been granted access or permission to enter the Promised Land, but they had to journey through the wilderness to get to that place. The objective of the wilderness is consecration; it is designed to wash the residue of your last season off you so that the revelation and information of your new season can properly cleave to you. But you can overstay your time in the wilderness; you can make a comfort zone out of the wilderness, and you can date and marry someone you met while in the wilderness. If this happens, you may find yourself in the custody of a wild animal (toxic person or narcissist) because the wilderness is not a place where you should settle down. Keep in mind that the journey from the Red Sea to the Promised Land should have taken the Israelites 11 days to complete. It ended up taking them over forty years instead. This was because they were not in the right shape, both mentally or spiritually, to enter into the Promised Land. This is to say that while the promises of God are yes and amen, we have to be in the right season (shape) to access those blessings. This is why the scriptures tell us to be renewed or transformed by the renewing of our minds (see Romans 12:2).

Some relationships are designed to get you out of shape. These are the demonically arranged relationships we briefly spoke about. Remember:
1. God formed you.
2. Sin deformed you.
3. The world conformed you.
4. Now, you have to be transformed by the renewing of your mind.

Transformation takes place when we embrace, accept and ruminate the right information. This is how we escape one season to enter another. In the church, we love to shout, "It's your season," before springing from our seats and jumping as high as we can. However, faith without works is dead; this means that change is a product of intentionality. You will never be transformed while regurgitating and consuming the same information unless you chew or ruminate that information and extract a greater measure of revelation from it than you previously extracted. In other words, all of our church antics are nothing but powerless performances (also known as religiousness) if we don't do our due diligence of studying and applying God's Word. Don't mistake what I'm saying; you should jump, shout, dance, run laps—do whatever God impresses upon your heart to do, but never think that any of these are substitutes for studying or obeying the Word of God.

Every season has a shape. The same is true for our souls. Your soul will always take the shape of the season that it's in, and when you exit that season, your heart breaks; the heart is also known as the mind, biblically speaking, and it is the center or seat of the soul. We grieve every mindset that we leave behind, but this grief is not always loud or demonstrative. Sometimes, we experience frustration, pressure, depression or sadness when we are exiting or leaving behind a school of thought. With those beliefs, we simultaneously leave behind the people who are loyal to the seasons that God has delivered us from or promoted us to. This is a frustrating event, but it is also a necessary one. Once our heart breaks, it is then malleable enough to be transformed by the water of the Word. This is why God also refers to Himself as our Potter, while we are the clay. So, when we exit a season, we enter into the wilderness, and while we're in the wilderness, we experience some of the major storms of life or we can experience droughts; this is largely dependent upon the direction of thought we choose. For example, if we choose to be bitter, unforgiving and vengeful, we'll experience droughts. Droughts make our souls rigid or inflexible. This disallows us from entering into the seasons ahead of us, but if we continue on forgiving and loving the people who've hurt and disappointed us, our tears will cause our souls to become pliable. This is what allows us to enter into the next seasons of our lives. And again, our souls will take the shape of whatever seasons we're in. Stubbornness is the product of ungodly beliefs, pride and unresolved trauma; it causes the soul to become stuck in the season it's in. Humility, on the other hand, is the product of intentionality (prayer, Bible study, faithfulness); it is a decision that we make outside of our feelings, thus forcing our emotions to submit to God's will. This is why you should NEVER allow yourself to be led by your feelings. The point is—if you're stuck in a reality that no longer serves you, chances are, you've missed one or more of the "ways of escape" that 1 Corinthians 10:13 speaks of, but fret not! You are living under the cloud of grace, meaning you can repent and return to the will of God for your life. Please understand this—being outside the will of God doesn't necessarily mean you're in blatant sin. Sometimes, it means that God has better in store for you, but you've chosen the lesser.

There are thought bubbles inside of every season called storms. A storm occurs when we are captured by and locked in a pocket of thoughts that we can't seem to escape. For example, have you ever had someone to offend you on your job, and no matter what you did, you couldn't seem to stop thinking about the person or the event itself? If so, you found yourself in a storm of sorts. Now, understand that there are personal storms and there are corporate storms. A corporate storm is an event that is shared by two or more people. Then again, two people can experience the same storm in different ways. For example, let's say that both you and a co-worker named Emma are experiencing the same string of events in the workplace. Both of you are being mistreated and mismanaged by your supervisor, Mrs. Houston. Mrs. Houston doesn't care too much for you or Emma. In truth, she wants the both of you to quit; this is because she wants an office filled with women like herself (gossipers), and she believes that you and Emma are an abomination to the atmosphere she's trying to establish. Nevertheless, your overall manager loves both you and Emma, and she's made this publicly known on several occasions. However, she's rarely in the office, so you find that you're almost always subjected to Mrs. Houston's antics. To aggravate you and Emma, she rarely, if ever, speaks to either of you, she never celebrates your accomplishments and she's always trying to publicly humiliate you. To add insult to injury, Mrs. Houston has written you and Emma up for being five minutes late, but she's always given grace to everyone else, especially the women she favors, and some of them have been no less than two hours late clocking in. For you, this storm may be unbearable; you may find yourself thinking about your workplace drama day-in and day-out. You may find yourself wanting to quit the job, or worse. Emma, on the other hand, may not feel the same way that you do. Why is this? Her core beliefs may not be the same as yours. For Emma, Mrs. Houston's behavior, while offensive, may be somewhat flattering. You see, Emma's father used to say to her, "Anytime a person dislikes you for no reason, there's a reason the person doesn't like you. Chances are, that person is intimidated by you. Don't get mad; don't get even. Just thank the Lord for your upcoming promotion." Because of this, Emma is actually flattered by Mrs. Houston's behavior. Both you and Emma are experiencing the same storm in different thought-bubbles, but remember, every thought has a foundation. Demonic thoughts need something to prop themselves up on or plug themselves into. Your anger may establish itself on the fact that you've experienced women like Mrs. Houston before and you never got delivered from the belief that those women needed to be humbled by warfare. This means that those bubbles are still floating around, and any bubble that is not popped will eventually wrap itself around you. Understand that each bubble is comprised of a series of thoughts, words and beliefs, and anytime you find yourself locked in one of them, a bunch of old frustrations and offenses will surface. This doesn't mean that you have neglected to forgive some of the people in your past; it does mean, however, that you have neglected to destroy the beliefs that once led you into unforgiveness. Consequently, you will likely find yourself wrestling with unforgiveness time and time again. You may find yourself forgiving people and living in that freedom for days, weeks and months at a time, and one day, you may find yourself right back in the ring with an offense that you thought you'd overcome, and here's the thing—you did overcome it! But overcoming an offense is not the same as eradicating the system of offense and falling out of agreement with the spirit of offense.

Remember these truths:
1. Something can be offensive, but that doesn't mean that you have to be offended.
2. Something can be scary, but that doesn't mean that you have to be scared.
3. Something can be frustrating, but you don't have to be frustrated.

You get to choose how to feel. Sure, emotions are bubbles within themselves and sometimes, they surround us on every side. Sometimes, it makes more sense to get into our feelings than it does to ignore the events that are taking place around us. Nevertheless, if we are not careful, we can repeatedly toss ourselves into a particular emotion until we become emotional and not intentional. A good example of this is a woman who repeatedly becomes offended every time someone at her job doesn't do things the way she believes they should be done. If she's not careful, she won't just be offended, she will take the shape of offense and become offensive. In this, you will find that she will become easily offended and intolerable, in addition to doing and saying things that are offensive. Over the course of time, she will discover that the people in her inner and intellectual circles are moving outward or away from her, while more toxic and offended people are moving towards her. She will also notice that most people are going out of their way to avoid her. This will ultimately lead to more offense, which will then result in her becoming more offensive. She will lock herself in the bubble of offense, and instead of moving forward, she will become one of the tools that Satan uses to hurt, harm and offend anyone who allows her into their circle. She'll be that cantankerous co-worker or that ill-tempered Christian who drives people away from the church. She'll be that disagreeable neighbor or that crabby customer who terrorizes every store, restaurant or company that she patronizes. She'll be that hot-tempered driver who tailgates other drivers, all the while blowing her horn and throwing temper tantrums on the highway. She'll become that tactless teacher whose words will ultimately bring trauma to one or more of her students. She'll become that erratic ex who keeps looking for any and every reason to either call the cops on her ex or to take the guy to court. This is because she chose to comply with the spirit of offense until she became an offensive spirit.

Remember, if you want to progress forward repeatedly, you have to be willing to allow God to put pressure on your potential. You have to be willing to let God transform your thinking again and again, knowing that a transformed mind will lead to the destruction or rearrangement of some relationships. Never be more loyal to people than you are to your purpose. Don't be one of those Christians who becomes comfortable in mediocrity; don't allow your comfort zones to become your coffins. Keep growing and going. And lastly, don't expect everyone to understand what God is doing in and through you. Be sure to surround yourself with wise counsel, but know that they won't always align or agree. This is why there's safety in the MULTITUDE of counsel, after all, God will echo His intentions and instructions through the large majority. Don't choose the counsel that reverberates with what your flesh wants; always be led by the Spirit of God in all things.

SEASONAL TOMBSTONES

Whenever I find myself hosting a series of negative thoughts and emotions, I typically take time out to sift through those thoughts. I do this with the intention of divorcing or destroying any beliefs that may be producing those thoughts. I also try to file away some thoughts so that I can test them later. Like most people, I don't like feeling sad, offended, discouraged, anxious, confused or rejected. One reason for this is, negative emotions can totally consume an entire day or week of my time; that is, of course, if I allow them to. In other words, negativity directly impacts my productivity, so any time I find myself feeling down, I stop what I'm doing to address my thoughts or the issues that are impacting my thought-life. If I've experienced the same set of emotions repeatedly (thought pattern) regarding an issue, I stop addressing the thoughts and begin to target the beliefs that are producing those thoughts. Understand this—every thought is rooted in a belief and every belief starts as a thought. If you don't address the belief, the thoughts will continue to surface.

In the previous chapter, we talked about the shape of a season, but did you know that in order for you to come out of one season, you must be willing to sacrifice whatever beliefs that are no longer beneficial to you? What you'll soon discover is this—sojourners have many graveyards behind them, and in those graveyards are the beliefs that once held them captive. Some of those beliefs were good for the seasons they were once in, but those beliefs have expired. Then again, some of the beliefs were demonic in nature. Lastly, some of the beliefs are comparable to junk food; they came about when the sojourner's voids cried out for information and revelation, and instead of studying the Word, the crusader in question decided to stuff that space with information that was momentarily satisfying and beneficial. A good example of this is a person who wrestles with rejection and abandonment. Let's call this individual Colby. Colby buys a book about rejection from the psychology section of a local bookstore, and while this is great and it will definitely help him on his healing journey, the information in that book is not solid enough to replace the Word of God or make Colby whole. Colby needs to study the Bible as well, so while the book on rejection was good and needed, it is junk food in comparison to the Bible. What Colby needs is to kill some of the beliefs he has surrounding his past and his relationships with some of the people he knows, but the only way that he can truly destroy these beliefs is if he pierces them with the sword of Truth; this is, of course, the Word of God. Understand this—Colby can deliver a nonfatal blow to those beliefs; then again, he can completely eradicate them by piercing them at their core. And once a belief has been dismantled and destroyed, it then has to be buried. What does it mean to bury a belief? Simply put, it means that you have to study the truth intently and intensely on a particular subject; you must do this until you recognize your former beliefs as lies and false information. For example, let's say that you once thought the Earth was flat. You studied scientific articles that supported your theory, you went to a few flat-earth conventions and you've even published a few articles about the subject of your own. This would mean that the concept of a flat Earth was a deeply-rooted belief of yours. Howbeit, one day, you came across a woman named Sandra who both believed and promoted that the Earth is round, and Sandra has a lot of evidence to support her beliefs. The two of you passionately disagree at a round Earth summit, and without warning, Sandra says something that completely shifts your views. She opens her Bible and reads Isaiah 40:22 (ESV), which states, "It is he who sits above the circle of the earth, and its inhabitants are like grasshoppers; who stretches out the heavens like a curtain, and spreads them like a tent to dwell in." She points out a few more scriptures and lines up more evidence to support her beliefs. You go home and change the way you look at the concept of a round Earth. Before you'd met Sandra, you were always looking for evidence to support your beliefs that the Earth is flat, but you start looking more objectively at what you used to look at favorably. You study the evidence for two days, and when you emerge from your house, you've had a paradigm shift. You no longer believe that the Earth is flat. Do you know what you've just done through studying? You simply buried your former beliefs under facts. Sandra pierced that particular belief, but you had to drive the sword into it. After this, you took the time out to bury the belief. Any belief that is not buried has the potential to be resurrected.

Have you ever met a woman who'd boasted about being abstinent for several years, only to have her fall back into sexual immorality? This isn't too alarming, but it does become more of a surprise when that woman has been abstinent for five or more years. What happened? The answer is—in most cases (not all), the woman in question wasn't truly delivered from fornication. She'd simply studied a few scriptures, joined an abstinence movement and went to a few singles' retreats. Proverbs 4:7 reads, "Wisdom is the principal thing; therefore get wisdom: and with all thy getting get understanding." Howbeit, 1 Corinthians 8:1 states, "Now as touching things offered unto idols, we know that we all have knowledge. Knowledge puffeth up, but charity edifieth." The point is that she embraced knowledge, but she didn't dig into revelation deep enough to unearth understanding. Because of this, her flesh wasn't fully crucified in the Eros zone. There were still some beliefs lingering in that neighborhood of thought that should have been uprooted, dismantled and then buried. Then again, we're all wrapped in flesh and if we don't use wisdom, our flesh will lead us into some dark places. Understand that every thought or belief gives life to another thought or belief. When a series of beliefs form and unite, they produce what is called a belief system.

Every thought that you have is designed to partner with another thought; when these thoughts come together, they form beliefs, and when two or more beliefs come together, they set the stage for principles. Principles are the thrones in which rulers sit on. If you worship God in Spirit and in Truth, He will be seated on the throne of your heart; if you have ungodly principles, a strongman (demon) will sit on the throne of your heart, and it will establish a stronghold (pattern, habit or addiction) and turn your heart into its personal septic tank. "The good person out of the good treasure of his heart produces good, and the evil person out of his evil treasure produces evil, for out of the abundance of the heart his mouth speaks" (Luke 6:45/ESV).

Amazingly enough, the word "belief" comes from the West Germanic "galaubon," and it means "to esteem or to trust." To esteem something means to hold it high, therefore, a belief is a principle or a thought that is held above every other thought or imagination. In other words, every thought has to obey or serve your beliefs. This is why 2 Corinthians 10:5 reads, "Casting down imaginations, and every high thing that exalteth itself against the knowledge of God, and bringing into captivity every thought to the obedience of Christ." Notice it said to cast down imaginations and every high thing that exalts itself against the knowledge (Word) of God, and to make every thought obey the Lord (translated). Pay attention to the words "high" and "down" in this particular text. This helps us to understand that there are low thoughts and there are thoughts that we esteem above other thoughts, just as there are low imaginations and high ones. In this, God is telling us that ungodly, low-dwelling imaginations can and will rise up against some of the principles we've established, and when this happens, our assignment isn't to ask God to give us new hearts and new minds; our assignment is to study and show ourselves approved for the new hearts and new minds He's promised us. Our assignment is to also confront and pull down every ungodly thought or imagination that tries to make its way to the throne room of our hearts. And when we cast those thoughts down, we shouldn't just leave them where they are, we have to bury them under the truth, otherwise, they'll repeatedly challenge the principles and beliefs we've already established.

As a recap from Book One, our souls are comprised of our minds, will and emotions. The mind is three-dimensional; it is comprised of the conscious, subconscious and unconscious minds. The conscious mind is the waiting room of the soul, whereas the subconscious houses the the heart of the soul. This is what God told us to guard. The unconscious is the spirit of the soul; it's our life-center. It's also where our habits and traumas are stored. The subconscious is what we want to give the greatest amount of our attention to, after all, if anything invades our unconscious mind, it could only mean that we have been turned over to a reprobate mind. This is something only

God can do. The seat or core of your belief system (heart) sits at the center of your subconscious, and any information that you hear or read is auditioning for a role in your heart. The information that is currently in your heart is magnetic, meaning it attracts like information to it. For example, if a person believes that it's okay to engage in witchcraft, all the while professing to be a Christian, that individual's heart won't be fully guarded from any new witchcraft practices that starts trending. "That we henceforth be no more children, tossed to and fro, and carried about with every wind of doctrine, by the sleight of men, and cunning craftiness, whereby they lie in wait to deceive" (Ephesians 4:14). The person in question will do what Eve did in the Garden of Eden; he or she will "consider" the new doctrine. Because witchcraft and the Word are contrary to one another, the individual will ultimately choose one as a supreme belief (principle), all the while subjecting the other belief to that principle. Which belief will surface as the supreme one? The one the individual trusts in the most; this is the one the individual has to defend the most. Time and effort are currencies in the spiritual world, and whatever you repeatedly invest them in, you will value and esteem. Think of it this way. If you were a knight serving a king and you ended up going to war, would you protect the king on the battlefield or would you protect his bookkeeper? Would your answer change if the king was a valiant warrior who was far more skilled in the art of war than you were? Chances are, your answer would be no. If not, you wouldn't and shouldn't be trusted to guard the king. While the king is gutsy and proficient at warfare, he is still your king, so his life would be considered far more valuable than the life of his bookkeeper. Note: for whom this may concern: please don't apply the American "we're all equal" logic to this narrative; a dead king equals a kingdom without a ruler, and a kingdom without a ruler will find itself dealing with nonstop civil wars and invasions from outside kingdoms. This means that more people will die as those who lust for power attempt to take possession of the throne. The point is that our loyalties can never be divided; we will always choose a supreme ruler, and anything that's under that ruler will be subject to the ruler in question. This is why God said, "Thou shalt have no other gods before me" (Exodus 20:3). All the same, you can't defend two doctrines; you'll shield one, all the while, explaining away the other. And while God can fight for Himself, we are charged to fight the good fight of faith.

The second point is this—whatever belief sits on the throne of your heart as a principle will always invite other beliefs in with it. This is why it is so difficult for people to divorce some of their beliefs, after all, in divorcing those principles, they will set off a domino reaction in their belief systems. This would ultimately shift their perspectives and change life as they know it, so they'd rather be comfortably bound than to watch their worlds fall apart, not realizing that one of the greatest markers of growth is a changed mind. Think of it this way—imagine that you ran into your former best friend (let's call her Wendy). You and Wendy were close friends when you both were 8-years old, but it is now twenty years later, and you are standing just a few feet away from your former friend at your favorite restaurant. She almost looks the same, but it goes without saying that she's gotten taller, she's aged and she's gained a little weight. Nevertheless, her beautifully placed gap and almond-shaped eyes are still as vibrant as they were when she was younger. Wendy smiles at you as you approach her. The two of you hug, and once you've broken your grip, you step back and start talking with one another. To your surprise, Wendy sounds the same way she sounded when the two of you were kids. "I want ice cream," she says playfully. "My Mom said that I could get two scoops and I can get sprinkles because I brushed my teeth all by myself. See!" Wendy then opens her mouth, clinches her teeth together and shows you her slightly stained teeth. "And I'm gonna eat all my ice cream up because I'm a big girl!" You laugh hysterically as Wendy plants her face in the ice cream cone before fully finishing her sentence. "You're still silly," you joke as you examine Wendy's facial expressions. "Wendy!" A familiar voice comes from behind the counter. "What have I told you?! Don't talk to strangers! Sit over there until I get off." The woman then points to a booth that's nestled in the far right corner. It's Wendy's big sister, Rachel, and she clearly works at the restaurant. That's when you realize that Wendy isn't playing; she is not pretending to be a kid. Somehow, some way, she became developmentally delayed or stuck in a season mentally and emotionally, even though physically, she'd kept maturing. This is similar to what it looks like to be spiritually delayed. Again, spiritual or seasonal delays are often the product of us burying God's plans for us alive, all the while, befriending, marrying or moving in with the lessons we were supposed to learn. What does this all mean? It's simple. Someone can strike up a conversation with you, only to discover that you're still a babe in Christ when you should have been a meat-eating, fruit-bearing believer by now. In other words, you still sound like your last season! This is what happens when the only thing we've buried in our own personalized graveyards is our destinies and a few goldfish.

When I look behind me, I see tombstones as far as my eyes can see. Every tombstone represents a season that I didn't just come out of; instead, I had to die my way out of. I remember trying to intentionally escape some of the realities I'd tossed myself into. You see, as you mature in the Lord, you will find that your mind is a continuously evolving organism, and every time it shifts, something dies. All the same, every time it shifts, you'll find yourself pregnant with something new. And understand this—if you return to the mindset or the reality that God is trying to deliver you from, you will miscarry or abort what God has placed inside of you. Consequently, the tombstones in your wake will have the names of every opportunity that you sacrificed to maintain your reality. Howbeit, if you repeatedly say yes to God's will, allowing Him to mold you into the vessel He has designed you to be, you will find a graveyard of tombstones behind you, and this graveyard will serve as the final resting place of:

1. Who you once were.
2. Who you became over time.
3. Who you've pretended to be.
4. Who you thought you were.
5. Who you wish you were.

Each of these personalities host a series of traits that you've picked up over time, and every trait, characteristic and false personality you've adopted will have its own unique headstone. The most frustrating part of this is the fact that you've likely built relationships based on some of those factors, and any time you kill the part of you that people are connected to, the people you've formed relationships with will begin to fall away. Believe it or not, a lot of people abort this process when they start seeing some of the key people in their lives suddenly beginning to distance themselves from them or behave strangely. Nevertheless, it is never wise to choose the you they want you to be over the you God called you to be. All the same, people won't always fall out of your life instantly. Some of your relationships will slowly give up their ghosts over time; this is because the process of dying to self can oftentimes be slow, methodical and tedious, while other relationships will seem to disappear almost overnight. This often happens when the people in your life sense a change on the horizon and decide to leave you before you outgrow them.

What does your personal graveyard look like? Are your coffins above ground (still visible) or beneath the surface (out of sight)? Every relationship is a garment. Are some of your relationships too big for you; have you outgrown any of them or are you still holding onto the ones you hope to fit back into someday? Lastly, keep in mind that if you have a graveyard with no bodies, chances are, you're hanging with corpses. This is why some of their attitudes stink. Be honest with yourself and be sure to bury the beliefs that no longer serve you. Be sure to place a label on their headstones; this way, you won't attempt to unearth them. I learned to grow in my honesty with myself. I learned the hard way that we tell ourselves what we want to hear, and to get past this, we have to literally interrogate ourselves and trace our thoughts, beliefs, insecurities and motives to their very roots. Meaning, I don't accept the first answer that I give myself whenever I'm examining my heart or a situation. I will question and pick apart my thoughts until I get to the very root of an issue. This has allowed me to accept responsibility for everything that happened to the adult-sized me. This doesn't mean that I'm rendering a not-guilty verdict for anyone who's mishandled or mismanaged me, after all, I'm not their judge. God is. But since I can't change them, I focus on the person I can change, and that's me! This process has allowed me to funeralize some of the most toxic, non-beneficial, burdensome and flagrant beliefs.

24

Amazingly enough, I've noticed that every time I bury a belief, my life changes as my mind changes. In other words, I am progressing forward. So, when I decided to consider how far I've come, I was surprised to see the distance and difference between who I was then and who I am now. And get this—who I am now is not necessarily who I'll be later on, after all, we are continuously evolving and growing. Nevertheless, if and when I do have a growth spurt, I will be sure to give it the same level of commitment that I give any and every season that I enter. In other words, I'll honor the space I'm in, but I won't marry it!

Speed Limits

Every type of relationship has a speed limit. For example, toxic relationships often move incredibly fast. You meet someone, and almost immediately, you feel an intimate connection with that person, meaning you open up your heart way too fast for that person. The two of you then begin to boast and brag about how natural your connection feels, implying that God Himself knitted the relationship together. You then start solidifying your soul tie with that person by merging your plans, your family, your friends and maybe even some of your finances. What you don't realize is that you're moving too fast. In other words, you are not observing the speed limit of love; instead, the speed limit that you're traveling at produces both lust and obsession. And with these types of relationships, a crash or a fall is inevitable. Sometimes, the crash looks like an unplanned pregnancy. At other times, the fall looks like the discovery of a toxic trait in your spouse that the other partner refuses to acknowledge and/or address. In some extreme cases, the crash can look like you being stalked or harmed by the individual that you were in a relationship with. Either way, the relationship comes to a screeching halt once one or both of you finally sober up, leaving you both brokenhearted, frustrated and soul-tied to one another. To make matters worse, you may find yourself bearing the weight of a responsibility created by both of you, and from there, your former partner continues to reveal aspects of his or her personality that are not only toxic but dangerous.

Before we move any further into this lesson, let's talk about the different types of soul ties. In short, a soul tie is anything that knits or connects two or more souls together. What is the soul? It is comprised of the mind, will and emotions. This means that the evidence of a soul tie is:

1. A person is repeatedly on your mind, meaning, you find it hard, if not impossible, to stop thinking about that individual. Your mind is the center or core of your soul. Biblically speaking, the mind is also referred to as the heart. This is where all of your issues pour from. Another way to say this is—every issue of the heart is expressed through the emotions and ultimately through the mechanics of our will.

2. You are emotionally affected by the choices that a person makes or what takes place in that person's life. For example, if you get the news that your ex-boyfriend has won the lottery or is about to get married, and you immediately experience offense, grief, jealousy or entitlement, you are still soul-tied to that ex. If a former friend of yours posts to Facebook that her boyfriend has not only cheated on her, but he left her to be with someone else, and you experience joy, a sense of satisfaction or a false sense of peace, you are still soul-tied to that

friend, and the cables or veins that the enemy is using to knit the two of you together is unforgiveness.

3. Your choices are directly or indirectly impacted by the choices of another person. For example, your ex goes out and buys his wife a new car, and when you hear the news, you go out and buy yourself a better car. This means that your beliefs surrounding that ex are now expressing themselves through your will; it also means that your ex has a measure of control over your finances.

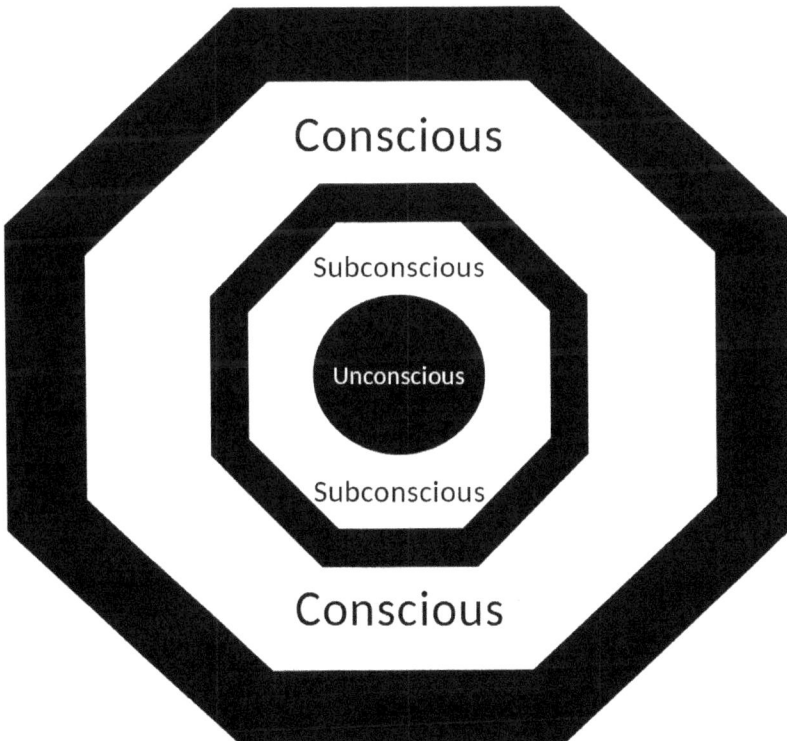

The diagram (previous page) will help you to understand how the mind affects both your emotions and your will. You'll notice in the diagram, the unconscious mind is the center of the image and the conscious (waiting room of the soul) is the outer court of the soul. The subconscious is the heart; this is what we are supposed to be guarding. In the diagram (below), the mind is the center of the image; this is your ocean, and in the midst of this ocean, you have your conscious mind (what's on the surface), your subconscious mind (what's immediately or just beneath the surface) and your unconscious mind (the depths of your heart).

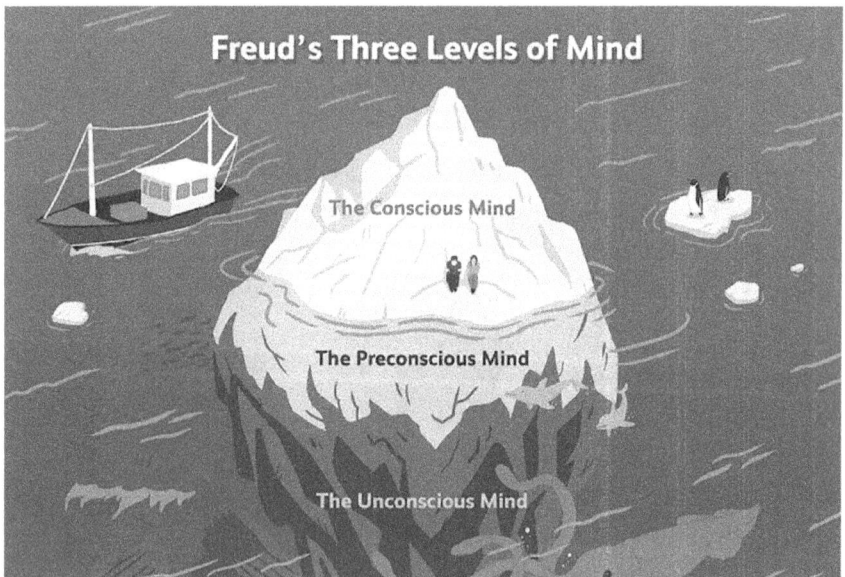

Freud's Three Levels of Mind

The Conscious Mind

The Preconscious Mind

The Unconscious Mind

The diagram above is the Sigmund Freud model. The diagram above and the following information was taken from Very Well Mind's website:

"Freud delineated the mind in the distinct levels, each with their own roles and functions.

1. The preconscious consists of anything that could potentially be brought into the conscious mind.
2. The conscious mind contains all of the thoughts, memories, feelings, and wishes of which we are aware at any given moment. This is the aspect of our mental processing that we can think and talk about rationally. This also includes our memory, which is not always part of consciousness but can be retrieved easily and brought into awareness.
3. The unconscious mind is a reservoir of feelings, thoughts, urges, and memories that are outside of our conscious awareness. The unconscious contains contents that are unacceptable or unpleasant, such as feelings of pain, anxiety, or conflict.
   Freud likened the three levels of mind to an iceberg. The top of the iceberg that you can see above the water represents the conscious mind. The part of the iceberg that is submerged below the water, but is still visible, is the preconscious. The bulk of the iceberg that lies unseen beneath the waterline represents the unconscious" (Source: Very Well Mind: The Preconscious, Conscious and Unconscious Minds/Kendra Cherry).

Please note that the preconscious and subconscious are one and the same. The model I created is what I call the Waiting Room model. In this, I liken the conscious mind to a waiting room, while the subconscious (heart) is the operating room. This is the space that all of the information that enters our waiting room (conscious) is trying to access. In my model, there are three levels or dimensions to the subconscious; they are the thirty-fold dimension, sixty-fold dimension and one-hundred-fold dimension.

Conscious	Subconscious	Unconscious
30 Fold	60 Fold	100 Fold

The heart is our personal Garden of Eden, and each dimension of the heart (subconscious) represents a depth. Some issues have shallow roots, meaning they don't need too much to grow; these issues tend to root themselves in the 30-fold dimension. These are what the Bible refers to as the "little foxes that destroy the vines" (see Song of Solomon 2:15). A natural example of a shallow-rooted plant includes ginger, parsley and spinach. These fruits and vegetables can be grown in containers in the home or they can be planted outside. Next, there are medium-rooted plants, which include garlic, onions and rosemary. This represents the 60-fold dimension of the heart. Bigger or deeper rooted issues tend to find themselves in this particular dimension. For example, most soul ties root themselves in this dimension, while idolatrous ties tend to root themselves in the 100-fold dimension. In the natural, the 100-fold dimension would host some of the larger trees, including olive trees, cherry trees and plum trees.

These are the issues that are so deeply rooted that they would require excavation to eradicate. This means that they often require the following to be uprooted:

1. Therapists.
2. Deliverance ministers.
3. Wise counselors (pastors, the elderly and mentors).

The mind is fluid. Imagine it as an ocean surrounded by a lake that's surrounded by a river. The ocean is the mind, the lake is the emotional realm and the river is your will. Once the mind is impacted, it creates a ripple effect. This ripple effect is a combination of your fears, thoughts and beliefs. This effect then makes its way into your emotions, causing you to feel angry, scared, surprised, excited, disgusted, calm or fearful. Now, understand this—you can contain a thought in the mind by overriding it with another thought, but the thought you overwhelm and override it with must be far more grounded or rooted than the initial thought, theory or belief that is threatening to destabilize your reality. You can also contain an issue in the emotional realm by not acting on your emotions, but this, of course, is difficult for most people. Nevertheless, if this wave is not dammed in or contained, it will express itself through the dimension that we call will. This is the one-hundred fold dimension; this is where a thought is given birth to in the form of a decision or choice.

The unconscious mind is the depth of the belief system; this is where memories, repressed thoughts, traumas, desires and habits are stored. This part of your mind is responsible for your automatic responses. For example, if someone hides behind a wall and suddenly jumps out, your response or reaction is a product of your unconscious mind. You'll notice that this is a somewhat instinctual and involuntary response. Another example of an unconscious response is when someone puts their finger or an object near one of your eyes. You'll notice that your eye will instinctively close without you putting much of any thought into it.

Now, let's discuss the different types of soul ties. They include, but are not limited to:

1. Covenants (vows, agreements, promises)
2. Hope
3. Financial soul ties (money mixing, debt, loans, offerings)
4. Idolatry (obsession, dependency, co-dependency)
5. Unforgiveness (hatred, wrath, variance)
6. Familial (parents, children, relatives)
7. Romantic
8. Corporate (church, job, communal)
9. Trauma Bonds

Believe it or not, you can soul tie yourself to someone by refusing to forgive that person. In this, you have unwittingly vowed to serve as a monitoring spirit in that person's life, and in some cases, you have decided to serve as a witch, a medium or an avenger in that person's life.

For example, it is not uncommon for people who are co-parenting to host hatred in their hearts for one another. This hatred is oftentimes expressed, for example, through the woman repeatedly taking the father of her child or children to court in an attempt to punish him and burn him out financially. She may rehearse in her mind that she has forgiven the guy, but every time she hears about him being in a relationship with another woman or that he's gotten another woman pregnant, she finds herself feeling angry and overly determined to make sure that he feels the added pressures associated with his decision to not clean up his life and either return to her or to be the father she wants him to be. This means that she may be romantically obsessed with him or, if she's not romantically obsessed with him, she might be obsessed with avenging her heart or the heart(s) of her child/children. This means that just about every decision he makes in the arenas of finance and romance directly impacts her as well. He may respond by going off social media and trying to keep his life as quiet as possible, but if he lives in the same city, town or community as her, or if they have mutual friends, he will find that the ripple effects of his decisions tend to find their way into her household, thus creating a riptide that will ultimately hit his home. This hatred may also manifest itself as entitlement in the man, whereas, he may repeatedly surface in his ex's life every time he hears that she's either attempting to move on romantically, she's making some advancements in her career or she's growing closer to God. In this, the man in question will use the soul tie he has with his ex to yank her back into his plans for her. For example, a child can serve as a soul tie between two people. So, the father of that child may suddenly file for custody or joint custody of his child/children simply because his ex has started dating someone else. This is the soul tie of unforgiveness, and please note that unforgiveness is not just hosting a bunch of negative thoughts and emotions for a person; it can also hide behind a series of positive thoughts and emotions, but it is often manifested through entitlement. So, the guy in question may have a positive attitude towards his ex (as long as she remains single). He may have said to himself that she is an awesome mother and a remarkable woman; these are the beliefs that he would be hosting in the 30-fold dimension of his mind, meaning, it's what's on the surface, but in the 60-fold or 100-fold dimension, he may be hosting thoughts that he is in denial of. A good example of this is—Craig has two daughters with his ex-girlfriend, Shayla. At one point, Shayla hosted a lot of negative emotions in regards to Craig. This was because he'd promised to marry her someday, but instead, he'd left her to raise two children on her own. Their breakup had been the result of Craig's inability to remain faithful. Nevertheless, two years after their breakup, Shayla managed to not only forgive Craig, but she made a deal with him to not take him to court regarding child support if he continued to support his daughters financially. Craig is a great father! He honors the agreement religiously, giving Shayla more than one thousand dollars every month to help with raising his daughters. He also buys clothes for them, gives them a weekly allowance and takes them on regular outings. All the same, Craig and Shayla get along extremely well! Every time he calls for his children, the former couple shares a few laughs before Shayla hands the phone to one of their daughters. All is well with Shayla and Craig; that is until Shayla starts dating Jerome. At first, when Craig heard about Jerome, he was a little uncomfortable, but Jerome wasn't the first man Shayla had dated since their breakup. She'd attempted to date on two other occasions, and those relationships had gone up in flames almost immediately, plus, she'd never introduced the men to her daughters. But something about Jerome was different. First and foremost, Shayla had been spotted around town with the muscular Jerome a few times, and the couple was always seen holding hands. This, of course, makes its way back to Craig. Craig confronts his ex, and she assures him that Jerome has never met their daughters, and every time she's gone out with her new friend, the girls had either been at school, at her parents' house or spending the weekend at Craig's house. To remedy this, Craig decides to stop keeping his daughters over the weekend, claiming that he's now having to work seven days a week. Things take a turn for the worst when Shayla changes her relationship status on Facebook to "In a Relationship." To add insult to injury, she then changes her profile picture to a picture of her and her hunky new lover staring at one another. This "love-shot" proves to be more than Craig can bear, especially since he can tell from the photo that Jerome is not only serious about Shayla, but he's madly in love with the mother of Craig's children. Realizing that the spot he'd subconsciously thought he'd reserved for himself is now occupied by another man, Craig suddenly begins to show up at Shayla's house unannounced, call at all hours of the night and complain about just about every decision Shayla makes regarding their girls. The two argue repeatedly until Shayla has no choice but to start setting boundaries around herself and her daughters. She tells Craig that he can't call her house after eight o'clock, he has to ask and inform her before coming to her house and he can no longer decide when and if he's going to pick up their daughters. "I need you to be consistent," Shayla says. However, Craig is not willing to watch another man take what he deems to be "his place." So, he continues to make co-parenting extra difficult for his ex-lover until something he witnesses on social media pushes him over the edge.

One day, Craig is scrolling on Facebook when he notices a video at the top of his timeline from Shayla's page, and the first thing that captures his attention is the number of likes the video has. With 763 likes and more than one-hundred shares, this video makes Craig's heart skip a few beats. He clicks the video, and it immediately begins to play. The video starts with a falling rose petal graphic that reads, "When a man finds a wife, he finds a good thing." When the video starts, Shayla can be seen walking down a long and elegant hallway. She's wearing a beautiful lavender evening dress that hugs her slender figure before loosely flowing to the ground in a train-like fashion. She's accompanied by two other women who are also wearing lavender evening gowns, but each gown is different, and no gown is as elegant and as regal as the gown Shayla is wearing. Walking in the center of the hallway, it becomes immediately clear that Shayla is the focus of this video. The flashes from cameras can be seen as Shayla looks ahead in shock, confusion, fear and anticipation. "What's happening?" Shayla can be heard asking one of the women accompanying her. "I thought this was a photo shoot." Suddenly, the rose petal graphic appears again, this time crowning the words, "A prudent wife, who can find?" After this, the video commences as Shayla enters a large and beautifully decorated outdoor venue. The women all move away from her as she looks around in confusion and dismay. "Hey Mommy!" The voices of Shayla and Craig's daughters are unmistakable. Shayla finally allows a lone tear to escape her eyes as her daughters rush up to her and hug her. The camera pans to show a crowd filled with both familiar and unfamiliar faces. Slowly, but surely, every woman in the crowd who's wearing a lavender gown makes their way to Shayla, handing her a lavender rose. The tears on Shayla's face begin to glisten as the lights from the lighting fixtures and the lights emitted by the cameras' flashes begin to submerge her. Craig holds his camera a little closer as he watches Shayla's mother emerge from the crowd. "What?!" he shouts. "That old bat never liked me!" Shayla's mother walks up to her daughter, and places her right hand under Shayla's left eye, wiping away the tears that are now threatening to ruin her makeup. "I love you," she mumbles as she clears the path for Jerome's grand entrance. "He's the one."

Dressed in a white dress shirt, dark gray dress pants and a lavender tie, Jerome looks more than amazing as he makes his way over to the apple of his eye. Craig sits up in his seat and makes an audible noise of disgust as Jerome begins to serenade his ex. "Forever is a long time ... that's how long I'll love you! That's how long I'll love you ... forever!" Jerome sings. His voice is not only masculine, but it also has an innocence to it that makes Jerome sound god-like. His presence commands the attention of everyone in the room. His large brown eyes are hypnotic, but as mesmerizing as they are, nothing seems to compare to Jerome's beautiful, pink lips. Craig tries to focus on the video, but the cameraman seems to be a little too obsessed with Jerome's lips, zooming in on them every chance he gets. When the cameraman blinks long enough to break Jerome's spell of captivation, he finally turns the camera back to Shayla. Her mother's attempt to wipe her tears away was obviously futile! Shayla has managed to fall to her knees, causing her dress to spread out around her as if she was kneeling to take the perfect princess photo. With her head in her hands and her long, dark hair swept up in a princess-like bond, Shayla looks like a Disney character. Her glittery nails shimmer as the light from the flashes surround her. The sound of her weeping is overshadowed by the sound of Jerome's angelic voice.

Craig lets out a sigh as what was once numbness suddenly begins to transform into fear and dismay. "She told me that she hasn't allowed this clown around my daughters," he mumbles as he kicks his shoes off his feet one by one. "Shayla, the moment I laid eyes on you, I felt the presence of God!" Jerome's voice can be heard coming through Craig's phone. "You are truly one-of-a-kind, and I'm gonna keep it real with you ... my cupcake, I love you with every fiber of my being! I couldn't imagine life without you. It's funny ... I was thinking the other night, 'Man, what was life like before Shayla?' And, in truth, I couldn't remember much. You are the answer to my prayers; you are the favor of God manifested in the flesh! And earlier today, I met your beautiful daughters for the first time, and they are just as wonderful as you are! I can't wait to be their bonus dad!" The camera then pans to show Shayla's daughters, with the five-year old jumping for joy and the three-year old shyly covering her face as she smiles. "Baby, I don't just want you in my life. I need you in my life! Will you be, not just my wife, but my help-meet, my sunshine, my best friend and my forever love? Will you marry me, Shayla Denise Rogers?" Still on bended knees, Shayla can be seen shaking her head in affirmation as she extends her quivering right hand to the man who has just become her fiance. And the ring that Jerome places on Shayla's finger enrages Craig all the more. The empress diamond on the band is the largest diamond Craig has ever seen on an engagement ring. "I bet it's cubic zirconia," Craigs snarls as he closes out the video. Three weeks later, Shayla is served with court papers. As it turns out, Craig is now suing her for custody of their daughters.

What happened here? Craig had a soul tie with Shayla that she was initially unaware of. This soul tie is called hope. Hope hid itself behind a lot of positive thoughts, but when another man entered into a space that Craig believed to be his rightful place or space, hope began to defer itself. Proverbs 13:12 (NIV) reads, "Hope deferred makes the heart sick, but a longing fulfilled is a tree of life." Oxford Languages defines the word "defer" as "put off (an action or event) to a later time; postpone." Inwardly, Craig once hoped that Shayla would remain single for the rest of her life, leaving a spot open in her life should he decide to return. Believe it or not, this is more common than we care to admit. Both men and women tend to tie themselves with their ex-lovers by placing them in a realm called hope, and to keep themselves from dealing with how they truly feel, they only acknowledge the emotions that are on the surface. This means that they tend to root their true feelings in the 60 and 100-fold dimension, and those feelings only surface when something roots itself as deeper or at a greater depth than our plans.

But, what if I ruined this love story by saying that Shayla's relationship with Jerome went past true love's speed limit?

We'd all love to believe that Craig threw away a good thing, thought the grass was greener on the other side, and now, he is getting his "come-uppings" as he witnesses another man value the woman that he'd taken for granted. And this very-well may be the truth; that is, if Jerome and Shayla managed to remain sober throughout their dating and courting process. Then again, if they love-bombed one another and soul-tied themselves to one another illegally, their relationship is likely doomed. Please note the following information about love-bombing:

> "Love bombing occurs when someone "bombs" you with extreme displays of attention and affection. Although it can be a positive aspect at the beginning of a romantic relationship, it can lead to gaslighting and abuse. Psychologists caution it might be a manipulative tactic by a narcissist or sociopath in an attempt to control you.
> Love bombing often takes place at the onset of a relationship. At the beginning of getting to know each other, you might view this person as charming and especially attentive. This person will praise you effusively, tell you they adore you, and often seem to emotionally attach way too quickly.
> If you find yourself telling your friends your partner seems too good to be true, they just might be"
> (Source: Very Well Mind/What is Love Bombing?/Barbara Field).

Notice that love-bombing is (in most cases) affiliated with

narcissistic or toxic relationships. These relationships are what fairy tales are made of (notice: we only see the beginning of fairy tales, but we will never know how Cinderella or Snow White's love story pans out because they are just that: fairy tales). This is why one of the most pronounced signs that a person is either narcissistic, toxic or demonized is when that person is moving at an accelerated rate of speed, and this isn't just associated with romantic relationships. When someone is in a rush to become your friend or place a label on their relationship with you, this is a sign that the person has an unhealthy soul. This doesn't necessarily mean that the individual in question is a bad person (per se); it simply means that the person does not know how to enter or sustain a healthy relationship with anyone. And please don't fantasize about teaching the person how to love you. Love is not an emotion; it cannot be taught, but it can be learned. The Bible tells us that God is love (see 1 Jon 4:8). Therefore, when a person says, "I love you," what the individual is essentially saying is, "I have God's heart for you." If the person does not have God's heart, it is impossible for the person to love or have God's heart for you. Howbeit, there are millions upon millions of souls who have never been engaged in healthy relationships with other people, and all too often, they will attempt to enter your life with good intentions and bad hearts. And by bad, I don't necessarily mean "wicked," I mean ungodly or unhealthy. This is what deceives so many people who walk away from romantic relationships, churches and friendships genuinely believing that they've been mishandled when, in truth, they are focusing on their intentions, not their methods. For example, it is incredibly common for a person to walk into a church and decide that they're home; they've found their tribe and they can now begin to build relationships with some of the people there. But having no history of healthy relationships, they make a lot of fatal mistakes in their attempts to build relationships. These mistakes include, but are not limited to the following:

1. They try to get closest to the most powerful people (leaders) in the church.
2. They try to get close to some of the people who are close to the leaders of the church.
3. They completely ignore what they perceive to be the "regular folks" at the church.
4. They attempt to flatter and love-bomb the people in their sights.
5. They attempt to rush into relationships with the people they want to fit in with.
6. They get frustrated and offended when the people they are love-bombing do not reciprocate their interests.
7. They leave the church feeling rejected, misunderstood and judged when, in truth, they simply went about things the wrong way.

Understand that church and/or organizational leaders are accustomed to people trying to flatter and rush them into relationships. Sometimes, people will even attempt to offend their way into a relationship with the people they want to affiliate themselves with. They typically do this by acting out or requesting/demanding a relationship with the people they are interested in building relationships with. Once they are in those meetings, they complain, love-bomb and then pretty much give the leaders their verbal resumes. They'll say things like, "I'm a good person to know. I'm truly loyal! I wouldn't hurt a fly! Anyone would be blessed to know me." The leaders soon notice that they speak more of themselves than the problems they claim to have. They'll even forget about those problems if they get the conversations they want. And again, they'll go way past the speed limit of a healthy relationship to create soul ties with the people they want to walk alongside. If this methodology works, they will be in place to sow the seeds they want to sow, meaning they'll begin to talk about everything that they feel is wrong with that church. But again, they are driven or motivated by good intentions; this is why they tend to be incredibly hurt and angry whenever they leave a church, a relationship or a friendship. All the same, healthy relationships tend to follow a slow incline (see diagram below) that resembles a staircase, whereas, unhealthy relationships tend to have a steady but slippery incline upwards (see diagram below) that resembles a handicap ramp.

HEALTHY RELATIONSHIP

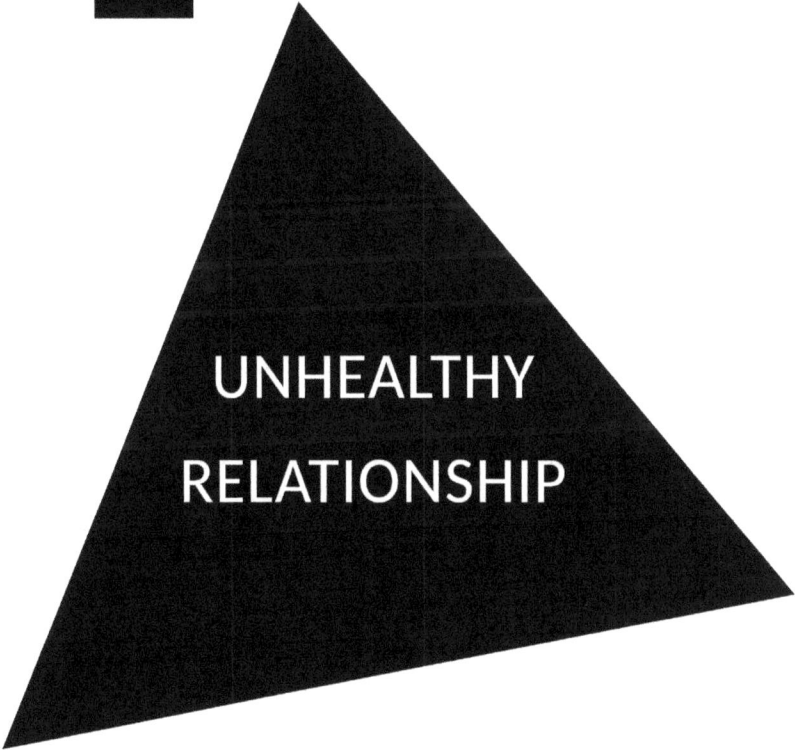

UNHEALTHY

RELATIONSHIP

Notice in the unhealthy relationship model, the

foundation is not level; this represents insecurity or instability.

Unhealthy, romantic relationships produce what we call the Notice that the first model resembles steps; this represents order, but the last model looks like a very steep mountain. It has no order, and in order to get up that incline, you have to go past the speed limit of a healthy relationship; this leads to the peak; this is what we call "cloud nine," and after the relationship peaks, it typically leads to a rapid decline. That is, of course, if you don't find a way to constantly refuel the relationship so that you can stay afloat it. Over the course of time, you'll begin to steal the virtue from others in order to stay atop that mountain. For example, your lover may have an affair with someone else, or you may end up sacrificing your relationship with your friends and family members in order to prove your love and loyalty to your lover. This is the result of what I call the "Cloud Nine Effect." What is "cloud nine," and where do we get the concept of this phenomenon? Merriam Webster defines "cloud nine" as "a feeling of well-being or elation." In short, the concept of cloud nine is synonymous with what we, in the western world, refer to as being "in love." It simply means to be in a blissful state often characterized by episodes of giddiness, sweaty palms, a racing heart and a queasiness that we often refer to as "butterflies in the stomach." But where does this statement originate? The following information was taken from the Farmer's Almanac:

"When you're feeling extremely happy or blissful, you might feel you're "on cloud nine." But what on earth does being happy have to do with clouds? And why cloud nine? This saying, which dates back to the early 1800s, was coined during a time when clouds were a topic of conversation. It was during this time that scientists and seafarers, including amateur meterorologist Luke Howard, first began organizing clouds. By observing cloud appearance and height above ground level, they were able to categorize all clouds into the ten basic cloud types we use today: cumulus, stratus, stratocumulus, nimbostratus, cumulonimbus, altostratus, altocumulus, cirrus, cirrostratus, and cirrocumulus. To make recording cloud observations easier, Howard and others also assigned a number from 0 to 9, to each of these ten cloud groups. According to their code abbreviations, zero represented the lowest clouds (stratus), and nine, the highest clouds (cumulonimbus, or thunderstorm clouds). It's from this that the expression "cloud nine" was likely born! (If you're on cloud nine, you'll be extremely high up, which also describes the sensation you may feel when overjoyed).

Today's meteorologists still learn these 0 to 9 cloud codes, but rarely ever use them. And since the numbers aren't used in public forecasts at all, most folks don't even know they exist and, therefore, don't realize this is where the saying "on cloud nine" originates from" (Source: Farmer's Almanac/Where Does The Saying "On Cloud Nine" Come From?/Tiffany Means).

Therefore, the concept of "cloud nine" is centered around being high or being in a state of perpetual bliss. But, get this—another word that we use for "high" nowadays is "under the influence" or "intoxicated." Then again, to be under the influence is the same as being bewitched. Let's look at a few scriptures.

- **1 Peter 5:8**: Be sober, be vigilant; because your adversary the devil, as a roaring lion, walketh about, seeking whom he may devour.
- **Galatians 3:1**: O foolish Galatians, who hath bewitched you, that ye should not obey the truth, before whose eyes Jesus Christ hath been evidently set forth, crucified among you?
- **1 Corinthians 5:11**: But now I am writing to you not to associate with anyone who bears the name of brother if he is guilty of sexual immorality or greed, or is an idolater, reviler, drunkard, or swindler—not even to eat with such a one.

Why am I sharing this? Because to be on "cloud nine" simply means to be under the influence of another person; it also means to be bewitched or to exchange the soundness of your mind for romantic delusion. Now, this isn't to say that the individual has erected an altar or created a potion to make you fall in love with him or her. This is to say that whenever you are on cloud nine, you are:

1. **Under the influence of that person's words.** For example, if the individual in question said to you, "I can't stop thinking about you. You are my soul mate, and I want to spend the rest of my life making you happy," those words have an incredible amount of weight and power. If those words are not challenged, or if you don't readjust the speed limit of that relationship, those words will make their way from your conscious (the waiting room of your soul) to your subconscious, and from there, they will begin to root themselves in your heart.

2. **Under the influence of your own imaginations.** I've said this maybe a thousand times—we often date and marry our imaginations of a person, but we divorce their realities. In other words, we fall in love with the people they are pretending to be, the people we have imagined them to be, the people they have the potential to become and the people they remind us of.

3. **Under the influence of the individual's potential.** All too often, we marry who the person has the potential to become, but when that person peaks prematurely and becomes satisfied in what we perceive to be mediocrity, we tend to sober up and run towards the nearest exits.

4. **Under the influence of a song:** Let's face it! Music is a powerful tool, and Satan often uses this tool to form and sustain soul ties. How many times have

you heard a song and thought to yourself, "Oh, this reminds me of (insert ex's name here)?" Chances are, this has happened more times than you care to admit. Understand this—most songs have something called a "hook." What is a hook? According to emastered.com, a hook is " a short line or phrase in a song that aims to make a song more memorable when a listener hears it. A great hook does this by utilizing a strong melody, rhythm, or lyrical phrase." A hook, in short, is a phrase that's chanted (let's call it what it is) repeatedly so that the listener can commit the song to memory. Remember, your memory is stored in the unconscious or deepest part of your mind. This is why Satan loves music so much! And one of the events I witnessed as a young lady was this—young and old men would ride through mostly poverty-stricken and seedy neighborhoods blasting their music. They'd have their windows down as they slowly drove around. They'd pass by women who were out walking, exercising or hunting for men. They'd then pay attention to how those women responded to whatever songs they were blasting. If a woman kept walking and did not turn to look at the driver, he would (in most cases) keep driving. This is because the hook in the song had no effect on her, and he didn't want to waste his time trying to talk to her. If a woman started wiggling like a fish on a hook, meaning, if she started dancing or swaying her hips, he would slow his vehicle down, stare at her and wait for her to give him eye contact. If she did this, he would stop his vehicle. Why is this? Because, believe it or not, the music accelerates the establishment of a soul tie, thus allowing him to "bed her" a lot faster. In other words, ungodly music increases the speed limit of relationships!

5. **Under the influence of a need**: If we can be honest, some people are in love with what you can do for them or what you have done for them, but they have no real interest in you as a human being.

When you're moving too fast in a relationship, you set the stage for the Cloud Nine Effect because the way our soul works is—when we meet new people, we have more questions than we have answers. The answers are supposed to be the substance of our relationships with those people, or they should serve as warnings to avoid those people. They can even help us to better understand where to place certain people in our lives. Amazingly enough, when we haven't developed the fruit of patience, we tend to want answers to these questions, and we want them fast! So, what we instinctively do whenever we're accustomed to toxic relationships is, we begin to subconsciously answer those questions through an event called fantasy. For example, let's create two characters: Boston and Florida. Florida has been dating Boston for two weeks, and she's anxious to know whether or not he's "the one." After wasting her time in a four-year relationship,

Florida is not willing to throw away any more of her time, especially given the fact that she is 37 years old. Howbeit, Florida doesn't want to scare Boston off by asking him a lot of questions, so she often imagines herself having the conversations with Boston that she secretly wants to have. One night, she imagines sitting on a blanket in the middle of a local park, having a picnic with Boston not too far from the sea. She imagines the sound of the waves crashing against the shore. She also imagines the two of them being on a relatively deserted beach, with only two other couples in the distance. Florida imagines the conversation going this way:

"So, what happened between you and your ex-wife?"

"What do you mean?"

"You told me that you filed for a divorce after only being married for three years, and I'm curious. Why did you file for divorce?"

"You're annoyingly cute, so I'll answer you. (Sigh). Okay, Sherry and I were going in different directions. I wanted to get closer to God, get into ministry and move our family to another state so that we can reset our lives. We'd gone through a lot in the state we were living in, and some of the memories seemed to haunt Sherry the most, especially the memory of how her father was murdered. I could forgive her for not wanting to move, after all, she had history in that town, and I didn't want to take that away from her, but what I felt like was almost unforgivable was how she responded to my desire to strengthen my relationship with God. I remember her looking at me one night when I was reading the Bible, and she literally said to me, 'I can't sleep with a Bible thumper.' I asked her what she meant by that and she literally told me that she wasn't going to have sex with me whenever she found me reading the Bible. Can you believe that?! And to make matters worse, I actually started complying. I would hide in the bathroom whenever I wanted to read the Bible, or I would read it in the car before coming home from work. But, one day, I felt convicted about it all and I started openly reading the Bible and talking about Jesus. And she honored her word! She wouldn't let me touch her for three and a half months! Not long after that, I discovered that she was having an affair with one of her exes, so I left and filed for divorce."

"Oh wow. How did you ever get to a place where you felt safe enough to date again, and why did you choose me?"

"The timing was right, and I won't lie to you. I considered passing you by that day when I saw you at church, but I just couldn't. Something in me told me that I was supposed to connect with you somehow, and now, here we are."

Florida then falls in love with the thought. What she's

doing is filling in the blanks, and again, this is extremely common nowadays. In other words, she's bringing herself under the influence; Boston didn't have to lie to her or manipulate her. After a while, this will become a major part of their relationship; that is ... Florida will fill in the blanks by imagining Boston's answer. This will cause her to not only quickly accelerate to cloud nine, but it will help to keep her high or under the influence whenever Boston proves himself to be someone other than the man she's imagined him to be. Meaning, she will spend many weeks, months or maybe years in denial. However, a healthy relationship moves at a steady and consistent pace. There are slight inclines in the beginning, but as the couple gets to know one another better, those steps will become bigger and bigger. In other words, they will grow together or, better yet, grow to love one another. The large majority of couples who follow the Cloud Nine Effect model will fall away from each other. Typically, what happens is—one or both parties will begin to sober up. This means that they'll stop filling in the blanks and they'll start erasing the answers that they themselves put in place regarding one another. From there, because of their experience with one another, they will begin to fill in those blanks with the truth. This creates the sobering effect and the inevitable event that we call "falling out of love." In a large majority of relationships, it is the man who falls out of love first because, according to 1 Peter 3:7, women are the weaker vessel. And by weaker, the Bible isn't just talking about physical strength, it's talking about emotional and mental strength. Psychologists say that women are better at recognizing their emotions, meaning we have an incredible amount of emotional intelligence, but we don't always have a lot of emotional strength. Of course, we can develop our emotional strength, just like men can increase their emotional intelligence.

Please note that an unhealthy relationship is filled with voids. A void, once again, is emptiness or shallowness. This means that the relationship has little to no substance. Healthy relationships are built one answer at a time. This doesn't necessarily mean that you need several years to build a healthy and blossoming relationship with another human being; it simply means that you need the fruit of patience. You also need the gift of discernment and a few wise counselors who can see your blind spots. All the same, you need a partner who has a healthy heart, just like you need a healthy heart. Here are a few signs and symptoms of a toxic lover:

1. The individual claims to love you in less than a month. The faster the person says this, the unhealthier the person more than likely is!
2. The individual keeps trying to sleep with you outside of marriage. This indicates that the individual has no self-control or true concept of what love is. It also indicates that the individual in question wrestles with insecurity and entitlement, and when these two come together, they produce pride.
3. The individual has a series of failed relationships, all

of which he or she takes no responsibility for. In other words, the individual blames his or her exes for the failure of each relationship, rather than acknowledging his or her role in the destruction of those relationships.

4. The individual shows signs of insecurity, jealousy and/or fear of rejection/abandonment. This usually signals that there are some larger and more detrimental issues at play in the person's heart.

5. The individual tries to merge his or her finances with yours, even though you're unmarried and the relationship is relatively new. People who do this often wrestle with what is commonly known as financial control and most of them are incredibly abusive.

6. The individual is dishonest or evasive regarding his or her intentions with you. This usually signals that the individual in question is not truly interested in you or the person may be in a relationship with someone else.

7. The individual (if you're dating a guy) has a pattern of getting women pregnant and then leaving them before his child reaches a certain age. This usually indicates that the person is a Cloud Niner (someone who falls in and out of love fast) or someone who is emotionally damaged. For example, some men leave the mothers of their children during the nursing and toddler stages because they begin to inwardly compete with their own children. Cloud Niners

typically fall in love fast because they almost always go the speed limit of obsession. They will plan to have children with you, attempt to move in with you and do most of the things that a spouse would or should do, but remember, the slope of toxicity is a slippery one.

8. The individual uses charm and flattery whenever you're talking to him/her, instead of helping you get to know him/her better. This is a form of gaslighting, and the purpose of this behavior is to allow the person to extract what he or she wants from the relationship (sex, money, a place to stay) without getting too invested in it. This also allows the individual to keep certain matters regarding his or her life private, especially those issues that could potentially change your mind about him or her.

9. The individual says things like, "I know you're going to leave me" or "Everyone leaves me at some point." This indicates that the person not only wrestles with rejection, but the person is manipulating you into swearing that you won't leave him or her. People who do this are oftentimes abusive and will often remind their victims of their decrees whenever those victims attempt to walk away from them. In other words, they use relational witchcraft to control their lovers. They will say things like, "You're just like everyone else! I told you that you were going to leave me! You promised that you wouldn't leave, but look at you! You lied to me!

You're just like everyone else!"

10. The individual buys you incredibly expensive gifts in the beginning of the relationship. The objective of this behavior is to make you feel as if you owe something to the individual, and if this behavioral pattern continues, it acclimates you to a certain lifestyle. Once you've adjusted to this lifestyle, the person will then use that financial soul tie to dominate and control you.

11. The individual repeatedly bashes his or her exes. This indicates that the person in question has not only failed to forgive his or her exes, but the individual may be conditioning you to help him or her to punish the ex or exes in question. This means that your soul tie with the person is 30-fold deep (if it even exists), but the ex's soul tie is rooted in the 60 or 100-fold dimension.

12. The individual puts you on punishment when he or she doesn't get his or her way. A good example of this behavior would be the individual refusing to answer your calls or threatening to break up with you simply because you didn't do what he or she wanted you to do. This behavior is designed to tame or train you to become a slave to your lover's emotions, desires, opinions and preferences.

Remember that true, Godly love has a speed limit. It doesn't move too fast and it doesn't move too slow. It moves at the pace of God's will. How fast does God's will move? It moves at the speed of your obedience (Apostle Bryan Meadows). This means that if you're mature enough to host a healthy and loving relationship, God will allow you to establish one. Note: if you're accustomed to having high-speed relationships that fizzle out in a matter of months or years, try this:

1. Heal. Get a therapist and keep getting therapy sessions until your therapist fires you.

2. Take dating off the menu until you've built, established and solidified your relationship with God and gotten enough healing whereas you can (1) choose a healthy partner and (2) healthily function in a relationship.

3. When your love for God has matured, make sure that you learn to love yourself with the love of God.

4. Love your neighbors as you love yourself! Build some healthy platonic relationships, and learn to manage your mind by casting down evil imaginations, and stopping the ripple effect of offense and fear before it crosses into the emotional realm, and finally, the realm of decision.

5. Pray for and surround yourself with wise counselors, and don't become too familiar with them! Honor them by helping them whenever or wherever they need help, sowing seeds into their lives and being there for them in their hours of need.

6. Get into your purpose! There aren't many things that are as satisfying as wrapping yourself up in

your God-given assignment!

7. Master establishing and setting boundaries, and then master solidifying those boundaries. After this, learn to stop apologizing for having boundaries.

8. Let someone love you, but don't forget to test the spirits behind every person who attempts to enter your life. Remember, keep each person in your intellectual space until God confirms through their fruits and patterns that they are healthy enough to enter your intimate space.

Demon Dung

Voids are hollow spaces in the soul. Where there is a void or dark spot in the soul, there will be demons since they are agents of darkness. Consider the following scriptures:

- **1 John 1:5:** This then is the message which we have heard of him, and declare unto you, that God is light, and in him is no darkness at all.
- **John 1:5:** And the light shineth in darkness; and the darkness comprehended it not.
- **Genesis 1:1–5:** In the beginning God created the heaven and the earth. And the earth was without form, and void; and darkness was upon the face of the deep. And the Spirit of God moved upon the face of the waters. And God said, Let there be light: and there was light. And God saw the light, that it was good: and God divided the light from the darkness. And God called the light Day, and the darkness he called Night. And the evening and the morning were the first day.

God is light; this is what the Bible tells us. Of course, He is not the light that the New Age talks about; He is the light of the world, and by world, the Bible doesn't mean planet. The word "world" here means system. But, wait! If God is light, why did He say "Let there be light" after He'd created the Heaven and the Earth? It's simple. God was filling the Earth with His glory. So, He wasn't necessarily creating light, He was spreading Himself out. In other words, He was depositing Himself into the Earth. What is a void? It's emptiness, darkness and shallowness. It means to be hollow or without substance. Simply put, a void is a dark space that has not yet been inhabited by God. Consider these truths:

- God is light.
- Wherever there is light, there is a revealing or, better yet, revelation.
- Light is the substance that fills the darkness. In other words, revelation is what God uses to fill our voids. Revelation, of course, is the hidden truths and mysteries of God.
- God is truth, meaning, He is His Word.
- The truth has to be sought after.
- When the truth initially fills a voided space (think of a human soul), that person is inwardly formed or, better yet, informed. This means that the person has information; this is what leads to transformation.
- When the person seeks God for understanding, that information is revealed or, better yet, it becomes revelation.
- Without the truth, a thing or person doesn't exist.
- When the truth has not entered the thing that has been formed, that thing will be deformed.
- When the truth is ignored within a space, the people have been misinformed or, better yet, conformed; this is what we commonly refer to as ignorance.

- When people repent and accept the truth, they are transformed by the renewing of their minds.

When a human being is filled with voids, those voids look like hollow spaces in their souls, and because we are multidimensional creatures, we can be filled with God in one area of our souls, but be completely hollow in other areas. For example, have you ever come in contact with a believer who is a strong intercessor, but that believer is horrible at managing his or her finances? Chances are, that believer has a financial void brought on by ignorance and/or financial trauma. Before we go any further, let's talk about the different spaces or realms of a human soul. Please note that a kingdom is a realm. World Reference reported the following: "Kingdom is a synonym of realm. As nouns, the difference between kingdom and realm is that kingdom is a nation having a supreme ruler a king and/or queen while realm is an abstract sphere of influence, real or imagined." But before we go any further, let's focus on this truth—the human soul is broken up into several realms. These realms include, but are not limited to:
  - The daughter/son realm.
  - The parental realm; this includes the paternal dimension and the maternal dimension.
  - The Eros (romantic realm).
  - The Storge realm (familial realm or, better yet, family realm).
  - The Praktor realm (job/financial realm).

- The Sophia realm (realm of skill, profession).
- The realm of self (identity).
- The Philia (friendship/platonic relationship) realm.
- The Ethos realm (realm of character).
- The Agape realm (God's throne/spiritual realm).

Again, this is not a complete list of the realms found in a soul. Remember, each of these realms has dimensions (heights and depths). Going back to the plant example, a seed can root itself in the 30-fold dimension of a realm, or it can root itself in the 60 or 100-fold dimension. The deeper the seed roots itself, the bigger and stronger the roots. This is why some issues are harder to address than others. All the same, Satan's goal is to get as many demonic fruit trees into your soul as possible; this way, he can turn your soul into a forest or wilderness (a place of disorder and/or no cultivation), rather than a garden (a place of order). Note: the concept of a forest being a place of disorder versus a garden being a place of order originated through my pastor, Apostle Bryan Meadows. Remember that Satan's objective is to steal, kill and destroy.

Whenever you haven't invited God into a space, it will be without form and void, and darkness will be upon the face of it. Understand this—God is light, and darkness can't comprehend light; it runs and hides whenever light is present. This means that whatever is in the darkness will run as well. Of course, demons hide in voids or dark spaces.

This is why James 4:7 says, "Submit yourselves therefore to God. Resist the devil, and he will flee from you." When you submit yourself to God, you allow Him to enter whatever realm that is active in that moment; this means whatever realm you've opened to perform a function. For example, you may be building a website for one of your clients. In this moment, your Sophia realm is open. Let's say that your client is frustrating you. She's way too demanding, condescending and she wants far more than what she's paid for. The woman in question may truly be a broken soul; she may be filled with voids. Voids are cracks found in a soul, and within those cracks, you will find both darkness and the demons that live in the darkness. In other words, she's a demonized woman who finds satisfaction in belittling and breaking other people. Let's say that you've just gotten off yet another contention-filled call with her, and she is demanding that you redo the website all together. She likes the website, but her problem is, she wants to see what else you can do. You try to explain to her that you can't delete a site and present another to her so that she can choose between sites; she'd have to pay for two websites since she's asking for double the time, double the effort and double the resources than what you commonly use. However, she points out that nowhere in your contractual agreement with her does it say that she can't have options. "Your contract says, and I quote, 'Designer will revise website until Client is satisfied.'" Howbeit, you've revised her site several times and you've come to the conclusion that she cannot be satisfied (demons have the appetite of a bottomless pit). In that moment, you realize that you have likely wasted three weeks of your time because you can't keep putting your other clients' projects off to meet the demands of a person who wants more than what she's paid for. So, you pray about it. A few hours later, an idea enters your mind. You suddenly remember the frequently asked questions tab on your website, and one of the questions posted is, "How many revisions can I get to a website?" To which, the answer you posted is, "You can get unlimited revisions just as long as they are to the template you initially approved during our consultation process. Also, keep in mind that a revision is not a new request, meaning, you can't send in additional information. A revision constitutes a change of font, the realigning of images on a single page and the editing of any content provided by us." You excitedly copy this rule and paste it into an email you intend to send your client. You also include a link to the page that is posted on your website. As you're writing your letter to her, the Lord impresses upon your heart to be kind, but brace yourself for a counterattack from her. So, you send the email, and fifteen minutes later, your business line starts ringing. "Hello, Jane Doe Express; how can I help you?" You clear your throat and prepare yourself mentally, emotionally and spiritually for your client's narcissism. "You listen to me," she shouts. "I paid you over a thousand dollars to design this website for me, and you're going to do exactly what I asked! I want options, and either you give them to me or give me back my money!" She finishes up by huffing and puffing on the phone as she awaits your response. "Mrs. Karen," you say, interrupting her loud breathing. "Can I speak now?" Karen is angered all the more. "Speak! But don't waste my time! I've wasted enough time with you and your incompetent company!" You say a silent prayer as you wait for her to finish berating you. "Okay, thank you for allowing me to speak. I understand your concerns, and I sincerely wish that we could accommodate all of your requests and changes, but unfortunately, we allot a certain amount of time to our clients; this allows us to keep our costs down while keeping our clients happy. At this time, we'd like to sincerely apologize for wasting your time, but keep in mind that our time is equally valuable, just as the resources we used to create this dynamic website of yours. Howbeit, we've come to the realization that we have exhausted our resources and we've given you nearly three times the amount of time that we give our other very satisfied clients. It appears that we cannot satisfy you, and for this, we apologize. So, with that being said, we are prepared to offer you a partial refund. As a reminder, our contract states that you are not just paying for a website, but you are paying for our time, and if a designer has invested more than seven days on a project, the designer is entitled to fifty percent of the fees paid by the client, plus, we will hold on to our consultation fee of $250. The consultation fee is only dismissed upon the completion of an order, and since you have chosen to terminate the process, we are entitled to the consultation fee. This means that we will be keeping $750 of the $1000 paid. You will receive a refund of $250, and the payment will be returned to the credit card we have on file for you. Again, we offer our sincerest apologies, and you can expect this refund to be processed in less than thirty minutes." Before Mrs. Karen can respond, you bid her farewell and hang up the line. Less than a minute later, your phone rings again. You chuckle as you answer the line. "Jane Doe Express; how can we assist you today?" Karen's voice interrupts your pleasant greeting, "You listen to me, you ignorant, worthless waste of space! You will refund me all of my money or I will see you in court! I'll also leave you bad reviews! You don't want to mess with me! I know powerful people!" You sit up in your chair and adjust your earpiece. "Mrs. Karen, another clause in our contract states that you are not allowed to mentally or verbally abuse our staff, and calling me out of my name falls under the category of abuse; this allows me to not only terminate your contract, but deny you a refund. I've presented the options to you. You said yourself that you like the website, so the issue is not incompetency on our end. The issue is you want what we've never offered you; that is more time and resources, and we simply cannot give them to you. As I mentioned before, we are well prepared to offer you a partial refund, and if you'd like to take us to court, we happily welcome you to retain an attorney, and I will send you the contact information of our attorney so you can give that information to your attorney. We will no longer accept any calls from you because you've been incredibly abusive towards our staff. I'll give you the option again. Do you want to keep the website as it is, or would you like a refund? If you refuse these options, we will process you a partial refund and await a response from your attorney. Please note that we will counter sue for the full amount, given the fact that we've completed your website three times, and each time, you've demanded more changes. Plus, we will counter sue for attorney's fees. Don't be loud or abusive; the choice is yours!" With those words, Karen begins to use profanity and you disconnect the line. She immediately calls you back from a different phone number and says, "Don't refund me! I need this website! Just finish the contact page, and you and I are done! I never want to work with you or hear from you again! Is that understood?!" You agree and hang up the line. I know this story was probably triggering for some, but it's a real example of what graphic and web designers go through. What happened here? How did you manage to get rid of Karen? You submitted yourself to God and resisted the temptations of the enemy. Satan wanted to offend you and get you to berate, condescend and retaliate against Karen, but you remained calm, professional and kind throughout the ordeal. In other words, you continually shined the light of God. Consequently, Satan had to flee from you. What happened here was your Sophia realm was under attack. Believe it or not, this is a very effective attack against the creative. A lot of designers close their businesses after dealing with a handful of clients like Karen. They opt to work 9-5 jobs because they did not involve God in their transactions, and consequently, they ended up being held captive by a demonized woman or man for months, and even after they'd done everything their clients demanded, the clients still weren't satisfied and left them bad reviews. But, you took the James 4:7 route, causing Satan to see the light of God radiating through your words, and it was too much for him to bear, so he fled. What God was helping you to do is set boundaries. A boundary isn't just an invisible line or a loudly spoken "no," it is a warning. Another word for "boundary" is "standard." In this, God is saying, "Raise your standards" or "Erect a wall." Understand this—bound people hate boundaries because, believe it or not, devils are terrified of legalities that they themselves did not create. This is because it puts them at the person's mercy that they were assigned to attack. Let's say that you finished Mrs. Karen's website an hour later and sent her all of her passwords; you even sent her info on how to manage and maintain her site. You then closed her order and mentally prepared yourself for a bad review, but she never writes or posts it because you'd effectively warred well in the spirit. "For we do not wrestle against flesh and blood, but against principalities, against powers, against the rulers of the darkness of this age, against spiritual hosts of wickedness in the heavenly places" (Ephesians 6:12).

Every time you invite God into a void, that space fills with His light (revelation/glory) and demons cannot inhabit that space. And please note that demons aren't invisible people-like creatures with hideous faces and evil agendas; each demon is an embodiment of its assignment. For example, a demon of rage isn't just an entity that causes a person to feel angry, it is rage itself (the perspective, the attitude, the energy and the expression). When it enters a soul, it begins the process of mixing the entirety of its being with the personality of the person. It does this by destabilizing the person's faith. How does it accomplish this feat? It poops. I don't mean that it literally defecates, I mean that it expresses itself through a person. This poop is what we call toxins. When a person has more demon poop (toxin) in a particular realm than that person has revelation, that person will be considered toxic in that area. For example, Jane may be great at paying her bills and managing her money; this means that the Praktor realm (the realm that deals with finances) is swept, put in order and it is filled with light or revelation. However, Jane may be a horrible friend; she's always speaking reproachfully about her friends and she is always competing with them. This means that there is a void in the Philia section of Jane's soul, and in that void, you will find the devils of gossip, slander, envy, jealousy and a host of other demonic characters. These characters produce characteristics. Of course, toxicity is more than a product of demonic bondage, it's a product of an evil heart. It goes without saying that an evil heart attracts demonic spirits and not the other way around. And because Jane is financially sound and maybe even financially stable, her friends may find themselves confused, especially if she happens to identify herself as a Christian (note: not everyone who calls themselves Christians are true believers; some people are pharisaic, meaning they embody the same anti-love or anti-Christ spirit that the Pharisees embodied, but they identify themselves as Christians because they were raised in church and they are afraid of going to hell. Nevertheless, they are not saved). Jane's friends may watch her lift her hands in church, cry during the worship segment of Sunday service and volunteer at a host of charitable events, but at the same time, they may also witness her trying to control them, be condescending towards them and gossip about them to one another. This means that Jane is toxic in the Philia realm. And it has to be noted that each realm borders another realm. For example, the Praktor realm (job/financial realm) borders the Sophia realm (realm of skill, profession). So, how demonic spirits work is—once they've conquered one realm, they will begin to attack the realm that borders it; they do this so they can enter that realm. For example, the Philia realm is in the same neighborhood as the Eros (romantic) realm and the Storge (family) realm. Since the Storge realm is more on the outskirts of a soul, chances are, Jane was toxic in this realm before she became bound in the Philia realm, which means that the next stop for those toxins is the Eros realm; this is the realm of love and romance. This means that Jane will make a horrible wife! She may be controlling, vindictive and insecure. This is the result of her lacking revelation (the light of God) in those areas. And wherever there is no light or, better yet, wherever there is no revelation, there will be an abundance of ignorance and unanswered questions. And get this—Satan understands one of the mysteries of the human soul; that is—whenever we are immature or uninformed, we will have more questions than we have answers. And an immature soul is oftentimes lacking the fruit of patience. Consequently, the person will try to find something to fill that void with to satisfy the hunger pangs that he or she feels in that area. This is why people turn to witchcraft and a bunch of demonic movements in their attempts to get answers. And Satan gives them just that—answers! Amazingly enough, he gives them a lot of truths, but in the midst of those truths, there will always be a lie. The lie masks itself with the truth so that it can enter the heart, and once it does, it begins to dig so that it can root itself. Remember, a little leaven leavens the whole lump (see Galatians 5:9). Some lies root themselves 30-feet deep, while others can enter the 100-fold dimension. Once that area of the person's soul has become a wilderness or forest, the demonic spirits then set out to capture and control the neighboring areas; they do this until the person becomes severely toxic or until the soul splits because of double-mindedness. James 1:8 states, "A double minded man is unstable in all his ways." This is because a kingdom that is divided against itself cannot stand! After all, the soul is a domain within itself, and the heart is one of the kingdoms within that structure. All of these parts should work together, but when a person is divided within himself or herself, that person will experience a lot of internal warfare, because the individual has two kingdoms at war within himself or herself. If it gets too severe, we will start seeing multiple personalities manifesting through the person, after all, the word "schizo" means "split" and the suffix "phrenic" means "mind," so schizophrenia is a split or double mind. The phrase "double-minded" means to have two minds or two souls.

How do we detoxify our souls? How do we remove all of the demon poop that has accumulated over time?

1. First and foremost, repent. This means to turn around. Remember, we can only walk with God if we agree with Him (see Amos 3:3).
2. Pray, pray and then pray some more! You need the assistance of the Holy Spirit to guide you in this journey, after all, it is a journey!
3. Study your Bible daily! You need the Word if you truly want to be free.
4. Get into a good, Bible based church, and be consistent with your attendance. (Note: don't just show up on Sundays, be sure to attend Bible study regularly).
5. Go through deliverance! Cast the devil out of those realms (kingdoms) so that you can give God His seat of authority in those areas.
6. Clean the rooms; you do this by getting yourself a therapist and scheduling regular sessions with him or her until your healing is evident! In other words,

don't get two or three sessions and then quit!

7. Fill the rooms. Studying the Word is a great start, but you need revelation in those rooms. Revelation means wisdom. The Bible tells us that knowledge puffs up, which means it makes people prideful (see 1 Corinthians 8:1). Howbeit, the Bible tells us in Proverbs 18:15, "The heart of the prudent getteth knowledge; and the ear of the wise seeketh knowledge." So, we are to seek knowledge, but we need understanding to anchor us down; this is why the scriptures tell us, "Wisdom is the principal thing; therefore get wisdom: and with all thy getting get understanding" (Proverbs 4:7). So, wisdom is the principal or most important thing, but to get wisdom or revelation, we are to continually seek to understand what we've acquired. This is because wisdom seeks after more knowledge, and a person who has more knowledge than he or she has understanding is a person who will have a lot of unanswered questions and pride. Once again, when Satan sees a question mark, he sees an opportunity.

8. Walk with God until you agree with Him. What does this mean? There is a stage of adolescence that we all endure in our faith walks, and it is during this phase that we must be more intentional about following the ordinances of God. This is because we won't necessarily understand a lot of what we're taught; this is why having a consistent prayer life and Bible study routine is so important. This means

that your flesh will want to go left when God is heading right, so you have the responsibility of humbling yourself (see James 4:10, 1 Peter 5:6, Jeremiah 13:18), leaning not to your own understanding and allowing God to direct your path (see Proverbs 3:5). After you've built a solid and sound relationship with God, you will find that you instinctively agree with Him, meaning, you won't have to force yourself to follow His lead; you'll do this both naturally and spiritually.

9. Be mindful of your relational diet; this includes what you listen to, who you listen to, what you watch on television and the environments you find yourself in. One thing I've noticed is that people who walk together tend to emit the same scent, and by scent, I don't necessarily mean odor. I'm talking about their attitudes, their presence, their beliefs and their goals. In other words, some of them have matching demons! Also be aware of one-sided soul ties, also known as parasocial relationships. Very Well Mind reports the following about these relationship types: "A parasocial relationship is a one-sided relationship that a media user engages in with a media persona." While they aren't all bad, if you form them with ungodly people, you are giving their demons permission to poop in your soul because your heart (mind) is one of the levels of your soul, and you won't be guarding it from them. It often saddens me when I see the number of seasoned believers who

are still following demonized celebrities.

10. Be intentional, not emotional. Never allow yourself to be led by your feelings; instead, be led by the Word of God.

Toxins can be extracted out whenever a person is intentional about getting his or her healing, and growing in the things of the Lord, and when that person is consistent. Meaning, the individual chooses not to quit when things get hard and the individual prioritizes his or her mental and spiritual health over his or her carnal desires, plans and preferences.

Sticky Situations

Let's start this chapter with a bold statement: demons are sticky. Why are they sticky? Because our souls are sticky, and by sticky, I mean that they have a measure of adhesiveness to them. Another way of saying this is—demons are magnetic; they are attracted to certain issues and traumas and they attach themselves to those issues. For example, the devil of rejection is attracted to a soul that feels rejected, but remember, we are multidimensional beings. This means that it has to find the area of your life that's emitting the smell of rejection. If you've been rejected or you feel rejected by a parent, the spirit of rejection will make its way into the parental realm; if you feel rejected by a lover, the spirit of rejection will wander around in the Eros realm. If you are enduring financial abuse, the spirit of rejection will burrow itself in your financial realm, and once it finds its way in, it will set up shop. Understand this—demons feed on flesh that has not been crucified. As it feeds on the flesh, it increases the size of whatever void it finds by increasing the size of the trauma wounds found in that void. For example, many leaders have made the mistake of putting someone in power who is not only broken, but the person is both demonized, immature and prideful. I've made this mistake myself and I learned a lot from it. What happens is—toxic leaders create soul ties with the people under them; these soul ties are what we call trauma bonds. They employ the following tactics:

1. Giving personalized attention to some of their most broken and loyal followers.
2. Giving false affirmation to the people under their leadership.
3. Prophesying to the people they like, all the while, ignoring the ones they dislike.
4. Mishandling, mistreating or even abusing a few people under their care in an attempt to use them as examples, in addition to making the people who they have seemingly "accepted" feel wanted, seen, appreciated and welcome. In short, they create the mean girls' clubs that once shut them out.
5. Encouraging rebellion against the organization they have agreed to serve, volunteer or work in.
6. Causing the people under their care to feel rejected by the leader of the organization, all the while feeling accepted by them.
7. Teaching those under their care to ignore or mismanage the people they dislike or feel intimidated by. They often do this by intentionally overlooking or ignoring a person or by passively insinuating that the individual in question is evil or demonized. Most people are sheep; they won't question why one or two people are treated differently than the rest. They'll just follow suit.
8. Directly or indirectly promoting the idea that the organization's leader is intimidated by them and jealous of them.

9. Directly or indirectly promoting the idea that the organization's leader is corrupt.
10. Pointing out the leaders' flaws.
11. Opening their hearts and even crying to the people under their care in an attempt to look like a victim.
12. Putting people on punishment, including their leaders and those under their care when they don't get their way.

Obviously, these types of leaders are narcissistic, and after they've successfully trauma bonded with some of the people under their leadership, they:

1. Attempt to create a subsidiary or sector within the organization they are charged to follow. This club or gang of sorts is typically comprised of people who are disgruntled with the leader of the organization or the policies/politics of the organization. You'll notice that these individuals will not fully integrate into the organization, but will instead create their own sector or clique.
2. Try to initiate a revolt or rebellion against the organization they are charged to serve. Rarely, do they launch the revolt themselves. Instead, they typically find the blind-warriors (goons) under their care. The blind-warriors are the people who are not fully delivered from high-level rebellion; these are the people who still struggle with unforgiveness, anger, bitterness—people who have violent tendencies. Narcissistic leaders will rarely, if ever,

directly ask these people to attack the overhead leaders (overseers) of an organization; instead, they will often manipulate them by crying to them about the leaders' behaviors, and then they'll further manipulate the person by saying something to the effect of, "Don't dishonor them, though! They are still anointed!" They do this to protect themselves, after all, Jezebel will never take the fall for anyone or accept responsibility for her/his own actions. Instead, should the blind-warriors respond with violence, Jezebel wants to go on record saying, "I told her to let it go. I can't believe she did that!" Of course, the narcissistic leader knew how the woman or man under his or her care would respond; this is why they took their grievances to them.

3. Disconnect from or abandon the people they used as tools once their agendas are completed.

What happened here? The individual put in power did not have a healthy soul, and amazingly enough, narcissistic people specialize in creating ungodly soul ties with others. Again, these soul ties are called yokes. And when a broken leader is given power over broken and/or immature people, that leader will cause the people to cleave to him or her before walking away from the organization or doing further damage to the organization. This is what I call stickiness. But before we delve deeper into this concept, let's establish this fact—the soul is sticky. The adhesive ability of the soul is called agreement.

- **1 Samuel 18:1:** And it came to pass, when he had made an end of speaking unto Saul, that the soul of Jonathan was knit with the soul of David, and Jonathan loved him as his own soul.

Like tape, the soul's adhesiveness can begin to weaken over time. To see what this looks like, find some tape in your house (preferably the tape used to secure boxes). If you can, rip a piece of the tape off and repeatedly touch the sticky parts. You'll notice that the oil on your fingertips can be seen on the tape, and you'll also notice that every time you touch the tape in an area where you've touched it before, it loses more of its adhesiveness. In other words, the person will slowly but surely lose his or her ability to cleave to others. This is what happens to the soul when we keep allowing the wrong people to touch our hearts; this is why God told us to guard our hearts. The less grip or adherence a soul has, the more clingy the person will become. What is the difference between clinging and cleaving? Cleaving is a natural and instinctive merging of two souls or bodies; it is the result of two people repeatedly and passionately agreeing with one another; it is also a product of respect in the areas they don't agree. Clinging, on the other hand, is the intentional pursuit or stalking of an individual that is birthed because of fear, entitlement, rejection, fear of rejection, territoriality and distrust. Clinging is a perverted form of or an alternative to cleaving. Understanding this, we can now understand why sex outside of marriage is being normalized in many countries and cultures. Satan understands that the moment we sleep with a person, regardless of whether we are male or female, we will become one (in the flesh) with that person. Let's look at a few scriptures.

- **Genesis 2:24:** Therefore shall a man leave his father and his mother, and shall cleave unto his wife: and they shall be one flesh.
- **1 Corinthians 6:16:** What? Know ye not that he which is joined to an harlot is one body? for two, saith he, shall be one flesh.

Notice that oneness or the merging of two souls romantically is not limited to husband/wife relationships. Apostle Paul said that the man who joins himself or sleeps with a harlot (whore, promiscuous woman, etc.) will become one in the flesh with that woman. Oneness refers to marriage, but not in a traditional sense of the word. It means that two souls (mind, will and emotions) have come into agreement with one another, and to solidify or seal their agreement (marriage), they have consummated their agreements through the shedding of blood (sex). Think of it this way. A man sees a prostitute walking around in a seedy neighborhood. He stops the woman and asks, "How much does it cost to have one hour with you?" The woman in question looks at the man and sizes him up. He's driving a Bentley and he looks well put together. "One hundred dollars," she says. What's happening here is what we call negotiation. The man agrees or enters into a verbal contract with the woman; he pays her the money and she enters his vehicle. At that moment, they have several agreements, which include:

1. They don't honor their own bodies.
2. They don't honor their own souls.
3. They don't honor one another.
4. They don't honor the laws instituted by the United States government or the government of the country they are in (that's if prostitution is illegal in their countries or states).
5. They do not honor God.
6. They are objectifying one another.
7. They want sex without commitment.
8. Idolization. She idolizes money; he idolizes sex.

When the woman exits the man's car, she will take a piece of him with her; the same is true for him. He will take a piece of the woman with him. This will affect both of their adhesiveness. Therefore, any woman who marries the man in question will notice that his love is not wide enough or strong enough to cover her; she'll notice that her husband objectifies her, especially when he's angry with her or when he's in the mood for sex. In other words, he will lack the ability to be wholly intimate with her, after all, objectification is the enemy of intimacy. If God were to highlight his soul under a black light (revelation), the wife would see the fingerprints of multiple women all over her husband's mind, will and his emotions. This is why it would be easier for him to divorce her than it is for her to divorce him; that is, of course, if her soul is not covered in fingerprints. I'm sharing this to say that the enemy promotes fornication because he understands that a man or woman who has had multiple partners will find it nearly impossible to truly cleave to another person; instead, they will cling to the people they marry. Clinging destroys relationships; it robs one or both of the people involved in a relationship of his or her freedom and peace, and it causes the people involved to question their own character. After all, if your lover repeatedly questions your behavior, your whereabouts, your friends and your choices, you will slowly begin to think that you are not a good person when, in truth, your lover is clinging to you because he or she has an inability to cleave. We don't just do this in romantic relationships; we also do this in every other type of relationship, including our relationships with our spiritual leaders, counselors and mentors. In truth, this is where a lot of what people refer to as "church hurt" comes from. It is the glue behind unrealistic expectations. Understand that when a person has been repeatedly broken, rejected and mishandled, because we are all created in love by Love, that individual needs, desires and craves love. But because our media promotes false love, most people don't understand that God is Love; this is why He tells us to seek Him first (see Matthew 6:33). Howbeit, we are naturally, spiritually and instinctively attracted to spiritual environments; this is why many people who reject and/or hate God are drawn to witchcraft. Therefore, when a believer is both a babe in Christ (new to the faith or immature) and broken, that believer will likely have an inability to cleave; this causes the person to become clingy. What typically happens is—the individual will find a church that he or she likes (let's say that this is a man to make this flow better; we'll call him Steve). Steve steps into a church for the first time and he feels welcomed by the staff and seen by some of the people there. Now, all he needs is affirmation and acceptance. But Steve was abandoned by his father, mistreated by his mother and he's spent the entirety of his life dealing with rejection and abandonment. This caused him to place himself in a lot of relationships, with each relationship weakening his ability to cleave to the people he should be cleaving to. In other words, Steve has trust issues. He has good intentions but a bad heart. Bad hearts produce bad methods. So, when the pastor graced the stage and preached a message that pierced Steve's soul, he thought to himself, "I've got to get to know this man!" Steve felt a connection with the pastor, but get this—the connection was a severed soul tie looking for something or someone to latch itself to. Severed soul ties act as lassos when they are split, but not destroyed. For example, idolatry is an ungodly soul tie. If Steve soul-tied himself to a woman named Deborah, and he made her his everything, their breakup would not deliver him from idolatry. It would only deliver him from Deborah. That soul tie would remain; that is until he came out of agreement with Deborah. Howbeit, Steve would still be an idolatrous soul, and just like Satan goes about seeking someone to devour, Steve would be on the hunt for someone to replace Deborah. He's not necessarily looking for someone to love; he's looking for someone to soul tie himself to. This is because split or severed soul ties are heavy when they are not anchored. This heaviness is what we refer to as loneliness. Loneliness is not a product of being alone, after all, you'll find more married people who are lonely than you'll find single people who are lonely. Loneliness is the product of an unfinished conversation. What this means is, every relationship and every soul tie is strengthened by words, and these words don't just solidify our connections with other people, they help us to assume, embrace or reject an identity, whether that identity is false, incomplete or true. This is why most relationships fail; people tend to pursue and soul-tie themselves to other people an attempt to continue conversations that they've been having with themselves and their former lovers. For example, a man may say to himself that a woman should be submissive, not question his choices; she should work full-time, cook, keep the house clean and refrain from complaining. This view or internal conversation was initiated by his narcissistic father, so when he met the first woman he'd soul-tied himself to, he'd attempted to continue this conversation by either telling her what he believed or by attempting to tame her. Note: by taming, I mean that he punished her whenever she acted contrary to how he believed a woman should carry herself. This resulted in a breakdown of the relationship; this breakdown led to a breakup. This breakup led to heartbreak. And from this relational dynamic, he began to build onto his father's principles, creating his own personalized tower of Babel, only he wasn't attempting to enter Heaven, he was attempting to enter intimacy using an illegal method. This is why there is so much sexual perversion in the world today. Intimacy has two entrances. The first one is a push and pull door. This is the one that requires intentionality and pressure; this is the door that leads to our relationship with God. It does not open on its own. Instead, it requires that we knock on it, and whenever God invites us in, we must put pressure on it. The second door is a set of double doors; these doors are automatic, but they won't open for everyone. They'll only open for people who have God's heart; these are the people who have been approved by God to enter into that space. But whenever we invite people in who can't seem to get those automatic doors to open, we allow them in through illegal principles or methods; we call these windows. "Verily, verily, I say unto you, He that entereth not by the door into the sheepfold, but climbeth up some other way, the same is a thief and a robber" (John 10:1).

Going back to the example of Steve, he's found a pastor who he wants to soul-tie himself to, but Steve doesn't want the responsibility aspect of a relationship. He wants the pleasure but not the purpose; in other words, Steve is accustomed to perverted relationships. Please note that perversion is not always sexual; the word "pervert," according to Oxford Languages, means "alter (something) from its original course, meaning, or state to a distortion or corruption of what was first intended." Steve wants to be the pastor's friend, but here's the caveat—Steve does not know how to have hierarchical or tiered relationships (more on this later). This means that he doesn't understand rank, protocol or honor. Instead, Steve equalizes every person in his life; this makes it impossible for him to be poured into. Another word for this is familiarity, and while this word may be offensive to some people, the truth is, there are different types and heights of impartations. You can receive an impartation from a friend, but if that friend is on the same level as you, that impartation will increase your territory (width) but not your rank (height). But to increase in rank and stature, you need someone who outranks you to pour into you, and you have to honor that person in accordance with their rank and position in your life; that's if you want to grow in rank. If you don't want to be elevated, you can continue building friendships with people, but understand that the moment you soul-tie yourself with a person who outranks you, that individual won't have the ability to pour into you because of how you've positioned him or her in your mind. This is what happened to Steve. He was accustomed to relative or non-hierarchical relationships; he's never been taught about honor or protocol, therefore, Steve has a habit of looking for the humanity of every authority figure he's managed to connect himself to. Consequently, Steve has unwittingly learned to usurp the authority of every leader in his life; this has led to Steve repeatedly being abandoned and rejected, causing Steve to become bitter, entitled and unsettled in relationships. And now, Steve has his eyes on a new pastor, and remember, he has good intentions but a bad heart. Steve says in his heart, "I will protect this man at all costs! I'll sow thousands of dollars into his ministry! I will never walk away from this man; I will be committed to him for the rest of my life!" These are Steve's intentions. And this is why he felt rejected and hurt when the pastor did not open his life to him; instead, Steve's new pastor treated him like he treated the rest of the congregants. He hugged him, loved on him, prophesied to him, prayed for him, but he did not open his personal life to Steve. Because of this, Steve left that church crying that he had been "church hurt" when, in truth, his unrealistic expectations had not been met. Steve wanted to cling to his pastor or make an idol out of the guy; this is the result of him having an inability to cleave. And yes, people can idolize other people, all the while, familiarizing themselves with those people. This is the stuff that church-splits, exposed videos about pastors and church drama is made of! Whenever you idolize a leader while familiarizing yourself with that leader, you set the stage for high-level disappointment and hurt. This is because you will repeatedly see that leader's flaws, and very few things are worse than having a flawed god. Don't mistake what I'm saying. There are many authentic church hurt cases out there, and God will judge them all. All the same, not every claim of church hurt is the fault of the church or the pastor. Believe it or not, there are a lot of cases that are founded on unrealistic expectations on the congregant's end.

Again, ungodly soul ties weaken our abilities to cleave to other people. When this ability his removed, demons use the black holes in the soul (voids) as their homes, and remember that demons are sticky! The spirit of rejection will attract rejected people to you. The spirit of pride will attract insecure, boundary-hating, prideful people to you. The spirit of control attracts rebellious and controlling people; it also attracts people who've relinquished their self-control to demons. Read this carefully—demonized people soul-tie themselves to immature people, broken people and other demonized people, and once they've secured their soul ties, they then lead those people astray. I've literally witnessed people coming into churches, soul-tying themselves to other congregants and then leading those folks away from those churches. This is why you should always test the spirit of every person who attempts to enter your life, regardless of how anointed they appear to be, how attractive they are or how successful they are. I've learned that Satan pays attention to what you want the most by studying the people you look up to. He then sends people in your life who mirror those people or have some of the same qualities and/or realities that those people have. His objective is to get you to soul-tie yourself to those people, and once you have done so, he will then use those soul ties to drag, lead or seduce you out of God's will.

Lastly, please note that soul ties have strengths; the strongest ones are formed when we cleave (not cling) to people; we typically do this in the areas where our hearts have not been touched. This is why people tend to cleave to the people they have surrendered their virginity to. This is also why people are oftentimes the most hurt by the leaders they once gave the most access to their hearts (think trust and intimacy). After heartbreak, most people have trouble cleaving, so they start clinging, and the people who have lost their abilities to cleave to other people tend to objectify the people they connect themselves to. This is what we call exploitation. Exploitation is objectification on display; this is when people connect themselves with your abilities, your gifts, your material wealth and anything they want to extract, all the while, refusing to connect their hearts to your heart. This is what many people, including Christians, do to God. They connect themselves with His hands but not His heart. They idolize Heaven, but want nothing to do with holiness. They perform for God, but won't pursue Him. They praise God with their lips, but serve Satan with their bodies. They have a form of godliness, but deny the power thereof. These are the people Jesus spoke of in Matthew 7:22-23 when He said, "Many will say to me in that day, Lord, Lord, have we not prophesied in thy name? And in thy name have cast out devils? And in thy name done many wonderful works? And then will I profess unto them, I never knew you: depart from me, ye that work iniquity." Note: by the word "knew," Jesus is referencing marriage.

Remember, to marry means to unite in thought. In other words, they performed for Jesus, but did not agree with Him. Their drew near God with their mouths, but their hearts were far from Him. They cleaved to Satan, but they clung to religion; they led people to church, but not to God.

Can God restore our ability to wholly and healthily cleave to other people? Yes, if we repent and follow the instructions that are laid out in the Bible, not just in performance, but in truth. What this means is we must know God; this represents our marriage to Him through agreement. We must understand God's Word; this represents our repeated pursuit of Him, and we must embrace the wisdom of God; this represents our likeness, not just through willingness but through our willfulness (obedience) which, of course, is a product of our faith. This means that we must first and foremost cleave to God by chasing and embracing His Word. In other words, we have to take whatever stickiness or adhesiveness that we have left and connect ourselves to the Most High God. Whatever we give to God, He increases. So, if we soul-tie ourselves to God, He will increase our ability to bond to others, but not without giving us the gift of discernment. This is our proverbial "way of escape." Without discernment, we'll fuse our souls with the souls of everyone who says "Jesus" without first testing their spirits. This is because, once again, the soul is viscid; it not only has the ability to stick to other souls, but we are created to connect with other people. However, our assignment is to also:

1. Test the spirit to see IF we should connect.
2. Test the spirit to see HOW we should connect.
3. Test the spirit to see WHEN we should connect.
4. Test the spirit to see WHERE we should connect.
5. Test the spirit to see WHO we should connect to.
6. Test the spirit to see HOW LONG we should be connected.

Sometimes, we meet the people God intended for us to connect to through other people. All the same, we sometimes connect ourselves to the mediums or mediators and not the people they were supposed to introduce us to. In other words, we tend to cleave to the wrong people, and then ruin the right relationships by becoming clingy and distrustful. Lastly, let me say this regarding romantic relationships. I typically give myself three days to see whether or not a man is date-worthy. My objective when I meet a guy isn't to build a romantic relationship with him or to even see where he fits in my life because he may be a trespasser; I don't know who he is initially, therefore, I've learned to test the spirit of the guy first. I do this by asking the following questions:

1. Do you believe in Jesus?
2. Where are you in your relationship with the Lord?
3. Who is your pastor?
4. How often do you attend church?
5. Do you have any wise counsel? Who are they?
6. What are your beliefs about religion, God and

relationships?

7. What are your thoughts about marriage?

8. How many children do you have? How many women have mothered your children? What happened in your relationships with these women?

9. How active are you in the lives of your children?

10. I don't believe or participate in sex outside of marriage. What are your convictions surrounding this?

11. What are your thoughts regarding female preachers?

12. Have you ever been incarcerated? When? For what and for how long?

Of course, I don't have to ask all of these questions whenever I know the answers to some of them. I avoid romantic talk, discussions about "us" and any talks that would cause us to feel all fuzzy inside. The objective is to stay sober since the large majority of ungodly soul ties are formed with and secured by untested words. Most people who claim to be in love are simply under the influence of their own words or the words of their lovers. But once those words are tested by life, responsibilities and disagreements, most of them fall to the ground. We should seek to build Godly, strong and healthy relationships that are not secured by empty words. Relationships built on statements like "I love you," "I'm in love with you" or "I want to spend the rest of my life with you" are cute, at best, but they have no substance. Once tested, they almost always prove to be conditional; this is not perfect or agape love. If you repeatedly soul-tie yourself to people who love-bomb you, your adhesiveness will weaken, and when you finally meet someone who's Godly, healthy and whole enough to love you, you won't have the ability to link yourself to that person because of all of the fingerprints on your soul. Remember to:

1. Cleave to God first, and let your strongest connection be to Him and Him only.

2. Test the spirit of everyone who auditions for a role in your life.

3. Heal. If you don't heal before you connect with another person, you will place the fingerprints of the people who've hurt you, abandoned you, molested you, mistreated you and persecuted you on that person's soul.

4. Test the stickiness of every soul that attempts to connect to your soul. Don't end up cleaving to someone who's clinging to you.

5. Don't move anyone into your intimate circle too fast. Everyone who enters should come into your intellectual circle; this is where you will get to know them, and if they are God-approved for your intimate circle, you can let them slowly make their way into this space. Don't rush anything!

6. Have boundaries and consistently enforce them. Bound people hate boundaries, but they love binding themselves to other people.

7. Obey God! Obedience protects and restores your

ability to cleave.

8. Grow up! Immature people cleave to themselves, and then get angry with everyone who refuses to cleave or cling to them. In other words, they want one-sided relationships; they want pleasure without responsibility. This is the very recipe for perversion.

9. Stop playing the victim. Victims attract predatory people. You are more than a conqueror in Christ!

10. After connecting with God, learn to connect with who He's called you to be, and not who you want to be. People who connect with their false selves or false identities typically repel the right people from them because they themselves have not yet learned to be the right people.

TABLE TALK

If you want new opportunities to open for you, you have to stop sitting at some tables. All the same, you have to understand that each and every table that you can possibly sit at has unwritten and unspoken rules, etiquette, benefits, and most importantly, each table requires a sacrifice. Of course, some tables require small sacrifices, while others are pretty costly, and by costly, I mean that you will have to give up something valuable if you want to sit at them. One of the greatest and gravest mistakes that anyone can make is to treat every table the same. For example, many of us grew up in a particular income bracket, and we had access to a limited amount of tables. Most of the tables we sat at had the same cultures, while others had similar cultures that we quickly adapted to. I immediately think about one of my childhood best friends. First and foremost, let me talk about my family's table culture. In short, we didn't have any rules because we rarely dined as a family together. My Mom worked two jobs for the majority of my life so she was rarely home. My Dad, on the other hand, was in-between jobs a lot, meaning he was almost always unemployed. All the same, he was rarely home with me and my siblings, so we had to prepare our own meals most of the time. My brother is two years older than me, while my sister is six years younger than me. I can remember that I was around eight

-years old when my parents started leaving us at home alone. This meant that my brother was ten-years old and my sister was two-years old. So, our days looked like this: I would go to the kitchen and see something I wanted to eat. I'd ask my siblings if they wanted some of what I was about to prepare; this way, I could cook enough for them. My sister always said yes, while my brother would say yes sometimes and no at other times. I'd cook, my siblings would collect their plates and we'd all head to different rooms to eat. We didn't eat together at the table because my brother would almost always do something disgusting and ruin our appetites or we'd all get into an argument. Our arguments were loud and they often led to violence, so we didn't dine together much. The only time we sat at the table together was whenever one of my parents requested or required that we do so; this only took place when that parent was at home and wanted us all to dine together. Funny enough, we didn't have any order, protocol or etiquette at the table. In many cases, we'd argue about something and then disperse to our perspective rooms. This is why I dealt with culture-shock when I'd visited and spent the night over one of my best friends' house; this took place when I was around 11-years old. I was pleasantly surprised and taken aback when her mother woke us up one Saturday morning and said, "Go brush your teeth so that you can eat breakfast." At my house, we always slept in, and when we woke up, we'd prepare food for ourselves, and most of the time, this wasn't breakfast food. We just ate whatever we had a craving for if we could find it in our refrigerator or we ate what was available. So, my best friend and I got out of the bed and made our way to the bathroom. After brushing our teeth, I followed my friend to the kitchen. On the table, I saw our plates already prepared. We had two slices of bacon, some oatmeal, eggs, cinnamon toast and some sliced fruits on our plates. I looked at my friend; for whatever reason, I thought she'd look as shocked as I did, but it immediately became obvious to me that this was normal for her, as her expression did not change. She still looked groggy and bothered. In the center of the table were bowls and plates filled with biscuits, more bacon and more fruits in them. In front of us were glasses of orange juice and we all had a separate glass filled with water. I waited for her mother to briefly leave the kitchen before whispering something to the effect of, "Y'all eat like rich people!" Not knowing what to do first, I waited for her mother to reenter the kitchen, along with one or two of her siblings, and I just followed their leads. Her mother bowed her head to pray over the food, and everyone else followed suit. I stared at them all for a second or two before lowering my head and closing my eyes. From there, I listened as her mother prayed over the food. Once she was done, everyone began to do something different. One person grabbed the honey; another person started eating the oatmeal and another person reached for the biscuits. I soon realized that there were no rules surrounding what to eat first, so I dug in. Once we were done eating, I waited to see what to do next. My friend grabbed her plate, walked over to a trashcan and emptied out the food she hadn't eaten. I did the same. She then walked over to the sink and began to wash her plate out. This was another culture-shock for me because at our house, we would just place our dishes in the sink, and whomsoever turn it was to wash the dishes had to address the dishes in the sink before my mother got off work. If the dishes were dirty when she returned home from her first job, we would get the spanking of our lives. Of course, I couldn't wait to tell my parents about the "rich behaviors" of my friend's family because I was thoroughly impressed. Thankfully, I hadn't taken my family's table manners to their table; I hadn't sat there and talked about how we did things at our house, nor did I attempt to exalt our table manners over theirs. While I had never been taught table etiquette or table manners, I had been given a few lessons on honor and respect, and this is what helped me to not dishonor the table that I was sitting at.

I can remember the movie BAPS (Black American Princesses), starring Halle Berry, Natalie Desselle, and Martin Landau. The movie was a ghetto fairy tale of sorts; it encompassed everything that many of us who'd grown up in the ghetto dreamed about, but it was completely misleading. In the movie, Nisi (played by Halle Berry), and her best friend, Mickey (played by Natalie Desselle), played two "hood girls" or better yet, the way the world depicts "hood girls" or girls from the hood (urban areas). Their English was poor, the women were uneducated and they dreamed about opening a hair salon/soul food restaurant combo, but they didn't have the funds to do so. They got wind about an opportunity in Hollywood, where they could be cast in a music video and win a large sum of money. Below is Wikipedia's description of the movie plot.

> "Denise "Nisi" (Halle Berry) and Tamika "Mickey" (Natalie Desselle) work at a soul food diner in Decatur, Georgia. Their plan is to one day open the world's first combination hair salon and soul food restaurant if they ever get enough money. Their boyfriends, Ali (Pierre Edwards) and James (A.J. Johnson), hope to one day own a luxury cab company.
>
> Nisi and Mickey hear about a contest for a video girl where the winner gets $10,000 and spend all their savings to fly to Los Angeles for Nisi to compete. On the plane ride there, Nisi reads a book on etiquette and she and Mickey discuss their new hairstyles, which are so tall they block the movie projector.
>
> Although Nisi does not land the dancing girl role, a man named Antonio spots them at the auditions and offers them the same amount of money to be in a different music video and invites them to a Beverly Hills mansion. Once they arrive, they learn about the real reason they were brought there, which was for Nisi to pretend to be the granddaughter of a woman the owner of the house, an aging Mr. Blakemore (Martin Landau), once loved when he was younger named Lily. They agree to the plan, but eventually grow fond of Mr. Blakemore and take

care of him and refuse to take his money.
Feeling guilty for deceiving Mr. Blakemore, they
plan to return to Decatur and leave a confession
letter for him to read after they are gone. However,
before they can depart, Mr. Blakemore is rushed to
the hospital. Nisi tries to confess to him at his
bedside but he silences her before she can finish and
passes away soon afterwards. Mr. Blakemore's
lawyer, Tracy Shaw (Troy Byer), informs them that
he knew all along that Nisi was not Lily's
granddaughter because Lily never had any children.
Back at the mansion, Nisi, Mickey, and their
boyfriends are preparing to return to Decatur. Mr.
Blakemore's lawyer arrives and read's his last will
and testament, in which he calls the girls his
"B.A.P.S", short for Black American Princesses, and
gives them some portion of his wealth. The film
ends with Nisi and Mickey opening their
combination hair salon and restaurant, which they
name 'Lily'z' (Source: Wikipedia/B.A.P.S.)."

This movie received a lot of negative attention and
reviews, especially by Black Americans because it depicted
a negative stereotype about Black people. It portrayed us
as ignorant people who didn't take life seriously, people
who rebelled against order and systems, but felt entitled
to handouts. In the movie, the women only became
wealthy after the wealth was given to them by a wealthy
White male. Obviously, not all Black Americans hated the
film. I was one of the people who thought it was
interesting at the time because I was a teenager who'd

grown up in unfavorable conditions. And from where I stood, it seemed that the only way my family would be wealthy was if one of our distant, wealthy relatives died and somehow left their wealth to us. I remember hearing about an uncle in Saint Louis who'd passed away, leaving behind three gas stations. He didn't have any kids, so my family had discussions surrounding who would inherit his wealth and property. Because we didn't know him personally, my mother didn't attempt to enter into that conversation; she just dreamed aloud around us, her children, about inheriting one of those filling stations. Nevertheless, as I grew older, I began to detest some of the mindsets I'd once embraced. This was largely because any time I'd grow in an area, I would experience the wrath of some of the people in my family. This is what is referred to as the proverbial "crabs in a bucket" mentality. All had been well when I'd listened to some of them talk about the relatives who'd acquired success, especially the ones who'd distanced themselves from the family. Amazingly enough, the ones who hadn't fully distanced themselves were often gossiped about and even physically assaulted because the general belief amongst broken and oppressed people is that anyone who goes outside of their understanding needs to be repeatedly humbled and knocked off of their "high horses." They didn't have to do anything to warrant these attacks; they were punished for having a thought, a belief or a principle that differed from someone else's. Eventually, they came to understand that if they wanted to live long, drama-free lives, they too had to distance themselves from toxic family members who felt entitled to wealth and pleasure, but hated the responsibilities affiliated with the two. They had to learn to be okay with being seen as the relatives who thought they were "all that" or the relatives who thought they were "too good to be around family." Unfortunately, this is the sacrifice that many people have to make before they can sit at different tables; they have to stop sitting at the tables that they are familiar with because what they are fed at those tables could poison their potential by poisoning their perspectives. I learned that most people who acquire a certain measure of success do truly try to have relationships with most of their family's members, but they have to pull away once they realize that many of their kinfolks think that they need to be hazed every time they garner another measure of success or rank. The point is that the movie, B.A.P.S., while entertaining, only seemed to fuel negative stereotypes about Black people and some of the unrealistic perceptions that "some" Black people have. In truth, it was more divisive than anything, but that's just my opinion.

The truth is, you can't go to anyone's table and begin to exalt your culture over that table's culture; this is true regardless of the rank or economic status of the people who own that table. If a rich man went to a poor man's house and sat at the poor man's table, it would be rude for the rich man to exalt his beliefs and cultures over the poor man's beliefs and cultures. He couldn't sit where he wanted to sit, nor could he expect to be served in the same manner that he is served in his own home or at the tables that are relative (equal in rank) to his own. He'd have to eat the food that was placed before him and honor the table manners of that particular table. As I detailed in Relational Acuity 2.0, I'd sat at two tables when I lived in Germany that I did not have the etiquette or understanding to sit at. In short, I was ignorant. Note that the root word of "ignorant" is 'ignore." It means that information is present and available, but you choose to ignore it. In other words, ignorance is a willful sin. I could have studied table manners, Germany's table customs and what silverware to use for certain dishes, but I didn't bother doing so. This is because I was untraveled and my relational intelligence quotient (I.Q.) was embarrassingly low. I was prideful, arrogant and just plain uninformed. I thought every other culture was inferior to American culture. What's worse is I brought with me the table manners I'd picked up from the limited tables I'd sat at. I soon learned that what I'd exhibited was the pride that many people from countries outside the United States have affiliated with Americans. Like the French, we are reported as being a prideful people who have little to no desire to learn anything outside of what we've been taught. Looking back, I can honestly say that my behavior, while mild, was loud and uncouth. I'd dishonored the tables I'd been invited to. Thankfully, Germany wasn't my permanent residence, because had I still been living in the place, there's no telling how many doors would have been shut to me because of my prideful ways.

To date, I've sat at many tables; I've dined with the wealthy and I've dined with the impoverished, and I've learned to take a lesson from the 11-year old version of myself. I've learned to watch the people at the table so that I could mirror their table manners, but more importantly, I've learned the value of a Google search before going to those tables in the first place. All the same, I get annoyed when I see a person who's been privileged with the ability to sit at a table that he or she normally would not be invited to, and that person begins to behave erratically or the individual dishonors and disrespects the culture of that table. For example, while in the Dominican Republic with some of the students from my mentorship program, we'd went to one of the restaurants that was on the hotel's premises (it was an all-inclusive resort). There were 16 of us at a relatively long table, and we were all talking amongst one another when the waiter made his way to our table. He'd asked us what we wanted to drink, and then he'd proceeded to talk about the alcoholic beverages that were available. After this, some of the women began to grow eerily quiet. As their mentor, I made it a point to pay close attention to how they responded to that particular moment because it was definitely a teachable moment. Howbeit, I also made it a point to not look and see who'd ordered an alcoholic beverage. Most of the women knew to order non-alcoholic beverages since this was a Christian retreat. Howbeit, I was confident that a few had simply shrugged their shoulders and ordered alcohol despite the theme of the event. I didn't say anything because I didn't want to make anyone uncomfortable. Instead, I waited until the next day to post a voice message in our group page about table manners.

- **1 Corinthians 8:13:** Wherefore, if meat make my brother to offend, I will eat no flesh while the world standeth, lest I make my brother to offend.
- **Romans 14:21:** It is good neither to eat flesh, nor to drink wine, nor any thing whereby thy brother stumbleth, or is offended, or is made weak.

Was I offended knowing that some of the ladies had chosen to indulge in alcohol? No, but the teacher in me wanted to ensure that they didn't limit the tables that they would be invited to, so I explained table manners in the chat. My passion is to raise up women who will sit at the tables of dignitaries, and I knew that this wouldn't happen if I'd allowed that moment to pass us by. I'd done the same with a sister in Christ of mine when we'd started hanging out. I was mentoring her, and we'd sometimes go out to eat. When she'd made it known that she wanted to order some wine, I told her that it wasn't a great idea. "Why?" she'd asked, looking intently at me. "For one, I am a leader; you have to be mindful of that," I said. "Secondly, I don't drink, and finally, I'm here to pour into you. Don't cheapen this moment." Now, I'm sure I didn't say it that way, but you get the gist of it. What was I doing? I was teaching her not to treat that moment and that encounter the same way she'd treated every other table she'd sat at. I did this because I didn't want her to throw away any opportunities that could be afforded to her by simply making one unwise decision. All the same, in the Dominican Republic, I'd recorded a ten minute lesson on table manners, and most of the women had not listened to the audio by the time we'd dined out again. Somehow, one of the ladies brought the audio up, and the ladies listened intently while I explained the concept of table etiquette. I told them that there were three things that could limit the tables they sat at; they are pride, ignorance and dishonor. No one will be impressed with your learned table manners at their table. All the same, when meeting a group of people at a table, you should consider the theme of the event so you'll understand the rules and etiquette surrounding that particular table. I gave the following example: let's say that I was in Dubai, which is a predominantly Muslim country, and I was meeting with a group of entrepreneurs who I wanted to invest in my company. We'd all met up at a relatively fancy restaurant, and while the people who sat at the table with me were all Muslims, the restaurant had pork chops on the menu. Let's say that as the women and I were discussing business, I'd noticed one of the waitresses bringing out a plate to one of the tables near our table. On that plate was a simmering pork chop; it looked better than delicious and it smelled heavenly. All the same, every other item on the menu looked unappealing. Should I order the pork chops, despite the fact that I am dining with Muslims? Absolutely not! While this isn't their table, the truth of the matter is, we're having a business meeting and I'm wanting them to invest in my brand. If I ordered the pork chops, the other entrepreneurs at the table would likely not say anything to me, but they'd be offended enough to not cut me a check. This is because in that hour, I'd exalted my preference over their convictions. I explained to the ladies that I'd order something else off the menu, and once the meeting was over and everyone had dispersed, I'd make my way back into the restaurant to order the pork chops. Sure, I could be prideful in that moment and say to myself, "I'm not Muslim! If they don't like seeing me eat what I want to eat, all they have to do is turn their heads or close their eyes!" And with this, I'd lose one opportunity after another, but I'd get to keep my toxic pride. "Wherefore, if meat make my brother to offend, I will eat no flesh while the world standeth, lest I make my brother to offend" (1 Corinthians 8:13).

I'm saying all of this to say—not all tables are the same. Every table has etiquette, rules and cultures. Before you sit at a table, be sure to study the protocol surrounding that particular table. Additionally, never choose your pride over your purpose. Even if your table's cultures are superior to the culture of another table, never exalt or promote your table's cultures at that table. For example, check out the chart (next page) to see some of the tables you may sit at, and what you should never bring to these tables.

Tables	Don't Bring
Grief	Talks about yourself, your victories, your plans, etc.
Victory	Sad stories, pessimism, anger, drama, news' stories, victimhood.
Ministry or Ministry Related	Worldliness, alcohol, drugs, discussions about sex, gossip, rumors.
Birthday, Baby Showers, Weddings	Discussions about yourself or anything negative (this includes talks about abortions, miscarriages or breakups).
Prestigious/ Wealthy	A poverty mindset; this includes the belief that the richest person at that table is responsible for the tab; fear, pride, envy, jealousy and an attempt to impress the host of that table.
Worldly	Religious talk; spiritual discussions, controversial beliefs (Note: at tables like these, you have to win them with your behavior; you have to become the embodiment of Christ).
Romantic (Dating)	Discussions about exes, especially negative talk; your entire life's history, assumptions, perverse speech, insecurity.
Romantic (Marriage)	Complaints, condescending or negative speech, suspicions, reminders, assumptions or anything that would ignite an argument.

Tables	Don't Bring
Poverty	Boasting about your success, riches and affiliations; excessive amounts of money, a full stomach.
Business/ Entrepreneurial	Pride, boasting, rejection, a low-balling mentality, your friends, your children, mediocrity, pessimism, an empty hand.
Reconciliation	Accusation, slander, rumors, demands.
Negotiations	An empty binder; pride, stubbornness, fear, a lack of knowledge.
Friendship	Drama, selfishness (this includes excessive self-pity), the same issues your friends have attempted to help you with (that's if you have refused to take their advice), pride, negativity.
Job Interview	Discussions about politics, religion or controversial topics; complaints regarding former jobs or former bosses, excuses, special requests and demands (that is unless you are at a high demand in your industry, and you are so good at what you do that you're able to negotiate).

Cultivating Kingdom Relationships

Proverbs 18:22 is one of the most popular scriptures in relation to single living. It reads, "He who finds a wife finds a good thing and obtains favor from the LORD." This particular text has been the topic of many teachings and theological debates, and I've noticed a trend. Married leaders tend to echo one another; they highlight the gender references in this scripture and teach women to not pursue men romantically. They point out the hunter nature that men have been equipped with, while single leaders, especially the males, often dismiss this scripture, pointing out the fact that Ruth pursued Boaz, and not the other way around. Regardless of where you stand in this argument, please know this—everything that is good and Godly has to be pursued, including God Himself.

- **Jeremiah 29:11:** And ye shall seek me, and find me, when ye shall search for me with all your heart.
- **Isaiah 55:6:** Seek ye the LORD while he may be found, call ye upon him while he is near.
- **Psalm 105:4:** Seek the LORD, and his strength: seek his face evermore.

If you're not familiar with the story of Ruth, please read Ruth 1. In truth, Ruth hadn't taken a traditional route. At that space in time, the Israelites were still under the

Mosaic Law. Deuteronomy 25:5 gives the specifics of this particular law; it reads, "If brothers dwell together, and one of them dies and has no son, the wife of the dead man shall not be married outside the family to a stranger. Her husband's brother shall go in to her and take her as his wife and perform the duty of a husband's brother to her." The Bible mentions that in order for the surviving male sibling to fall under this particular law, he had to be living with his brother prior to his passing. This means that this scripture actually referenced most of the Israelite men at that time since men typically did not move out of their fathers' homes. Instead, before they took a bride for themselves, they would have to go back to their fathers' houses and make room for their new brides. In short, their fathers would allow them to occupy a space in their homes with their brides. Only the women left once they got married because they would go to live in their fathers-in-laws' homes with their husbands. Ruth was a Moabite woman, meaning, she wasn't an Israelite, therefore, she wasn't expected to adhere to the Hebrew religion following the death of her husband. The reason Ruth pursued Boaz was because:

1. She'd expressed a desire to follow Naomi (her mother-in-law).
2. She'd expressed a desire to follow Naomi's God (YAHWEH).
3. She'd been instructed by Naomi to do so.

Ruth 3:1-9 reads, "Then Naomi her mother in law said unto

her, My daughter, shall I not seek rest for thee, that it may be well with thee? And now is not Boaz of our kindred, with whose maidens thou wast? Behold, he winnoweth barley to night in the threshingfloor. wash thyself therefore, and anoint thee, and put thy raiment upon thee, and get thee down to the floor: but make not thyself known unto the man, until he shall have done eating and drinking. And it shall be, when he lieth down, that thou shalt mark the place where he shall lie, and thou shalt go in, and uncover his feet, and lay thee down; and he will tell thee what thou shalt do. And she said unto her, All that thou sayest unto me I will do. And she went down unto the floor, and did according to all that her mother in law bade her. And when Boaz had eaten and drunk, and his heart was merry, he went to lie down at the end of the heap of corn: and she came softly, and uncovered his feet, and laid her down. And it came to pass at midnight, that the man was afraid, and turned himself: and, behold, a woman lay at his feet. And he said, Who art thou? And she answered, I am Ruth thine handmaid: spread therefore thy skirt over thine handmaid; for thou art a near kinsman." In this, we come to understand the reason Ruth pursued Boaz. She was making him aware of her intentions to follow Jewish tradition because, again, it was largely assumed that she would return to her country and her former faith. This is to say that Ruth's story isn't a great example of why a woman should pursue a man, especially given the fact that the only other time we see this behavior is in Genesis 38, where we meet a woman named Tamar. Tamar's husband,

Er, passed away, and being a Jewish woman, she continued to follow the Mosaic Law. She ended up marrying her husband's brother, Onan, and according to Genesis 38:9, Onan didn't want to get her pregnant because he knew that their firstborn would be considered the son of his deceased brother, Er, which, again, was the law at that time. So, Onan spilled his seed on the ground; this is what we commonly refer to today as the withdrawal method. This act displeased God, so the Lord killed him. This meant that the next brother would have to marry Tamar and produce sons for his deceased brothers. This would allow the brothers' names to continue in the Earth. But, Tamar's father-in-law had different plans. He'd promised to send his youngest son to Tamar after he was of age, and he asked Tamar to go and live in her father's house until then. He never followed through with his promise, so Tamar took off her widow's garment, put on the garments of a harlot (whore), covered her face and she went and sat in the open square. When Judah saw her, he assumed that she was a prostitute, so he petitioned her to sleep with him. You can find the rest of this story in Genesis 38, but the story ends with Judah getting his daughter-in-law pregnant. The news went out to him that she was pregnant, but he did not know that she was the woman he'd slept with, so he told his servants to bring her to him so that she could be burnt. Howbeit, when she'd disguised herself as a prostitute, she'd requested three things from him: his signet rings, bracelets and staff. Genesis 38:24-26 tells us how this story ends; it reads, "And it came to pass about three months after, that it was told Judah, saying, Tamar thy daughter in law hath played the harlot; and also, behold, she is with child by whoredom. And Judah said, Bring her forth, and let her be burnt. When she was brought forth, she sent to her father in law, saying, By the man, whose these are, am I with child: and she said, Discern, I pray thee, whose are these, the signet, and bracelets, and staff. And Judah acknowledged them, and said, She hath been more righteous than I; because that I gave her not to Shelah my son. And he knew her again no more."

In the aforementioned story, we see, once again, a pursuit. Tamar was determined to follow Jewish tradition, and like many women, she wanted to be a wife and a mother, and after tragically losing both of her husbands to death, she'd patiently waited for her new husband to arrive. She wanted to love and to be loved, and Judah more than likely wanted to protect his youngest son, after all, he'd already lost two sons. Howbeit, despite his fears and insecurities, Tamar was unrelenting in her pursuit of love, happiness and motherhood. This is to say that love can be grown and it can be found, but it cannot be made.

Love comes in varying heights and measures. For example, the Bible mentions "perfect love" in 1 John 4:18. Another term commonly used for "perfect love" is "agape," which means unconditional love or God's kind of love. There are four types, levels or expressions of love. They are:

- **Eros:** erotic; passionate love; romantic love.
- **Philia:** love of friends and co-laborers; brotherly love.
- **Storge:** family love; love from and to parents; love of siblings, etc.
- **Agape:** God's love for mankind; unconditional love; pure love; perfect love.

It goes without saying that agape is the highest form or expression of love. This is the love that makes us whole; it is the love that we all go in search of, but rarely find. Don't get me wrong; God loves us and we are wrapped in His love. However, most of us are completely unaware of this, so we search for what we already have. This is because we have come to believe that love is an emotion (more on this shortly). Additionally, God's love covers us, but we have to accept it in order for it to dwell in us. And, it goes without saying—Satan mimics or creates a generic form of everything that God created. This includes love, and this is what a large portion of people on Earth today have come to believe and accept as love. A few generic forms of love include, but are not limited to:

- Lust.
- Obsession.
- Co-dependency.
- Fetishes.
- Fear of being alone or starting over.

True love is deeply rooted; it does not reside in the intellect (conscious or 30-fold realm); it begins to blossom in the 60-fold (subconscious) realm, and it doesn't become perfect love until it reaches the unconscious (100-fold) realm. Whenever we are blessed enough to find true love in relationships, be they platonic, familial or romantic, most of us never get past the 60-fold realm because we've never been taught how to love another human being at this capacity. The same is true for the people we grow to love. Most of them don't know how to fully love other human beings, so most of our relationships with people are conditional. What's worse is—many believers today have an intellectual relationship with God; they have restrained Him in the 30-fold dimensions of their hearts, but they have intimate relationships with other people. This is the very definition of idolatry. Look at the charts below.

Dimension	30-Fold	60-Fold	100-Fold
Religion	Self	God	Mankind
Idolatry	God	Mankind	Self
Holiness	Mankind	Self	God
Realm	Conscious	Subconscious	Unconscious

Anything that is not established in love FIRST will be established in fear. For example, religion roots itself in the fear of man and the fear of hell. Idolatry roots itself in the fear of loss or losing; it is what we refer to as "survivor's mode." And faith or holiness roots itself in the love of

God. Understand that the love of God first begins in the realm of fear; this is why Proverbs 9:10 says, "The fear of the LORD is the beginning of wisdom: and the knowledge of the holy is understanding." Howbeit, according to 1 John 4:18, perfect love drives out fear. Again, this is mature love. And because most people are not intentional or patient enough to reach this height, they spend the rest of their lives in fear-based relationships, fearing that their loved ones will reject or abandon them someday. Remember, the objective is to grow in love until your love matures, and then allow God to bring people into your life who've done the same. Now, this isn't to say that you can't or shouldn't have relationships with people who don't truly understand how to love themselves or others; this is to say that your objective with these people is to place the right labels on your relationships with them, and to be sure that you don't give them intimate access to your heart. Keep this rule and your heart will remain safe: never give someone access to your heart who doesn't know how to guard their own.

But how do you know when someone truly loves you? How can we differentiate true love from its counterfeits? 1 Corinthians 13:4-8 (ESV) answers this question for us. It reads, "Love is patient and kind; love does not envy or boast; it is not arrogant or rude. It does not insist on its own way; it is not irritable or resentful; it does not rejoice at wrongdoing, but rejoices with the truth. Love bears all things, believes all things, hopes all things, endures all things. Love never ends." In short, your goal is to first make sure that the characteristics of love are displaying through you, not just in works, but in thought. This will allow you to measure what another person is offering you in every given season of your relationship with that person, thus, giving you the ability to accept or reject their offers, but until you are able to weigh their words, you have to keep them in the intellectual realm. Again, this is where a lot of people mess up; they bring people too close too fast, and this is because our culture has normalized this behavior. Consequently, we have a growing number of mental health movements and crime is at an all-time high. Plainly said, a person who does not love God cannot wholly and healthily love you.

"Anyone who does not love does not know God, because God is love" (1 John 4:8). One of the biggest fallacies of our time is the belief that love is either an emotion or a feeling. As a matter of fact, Oxford Languages defines "love" as "an intense feeling of deep affection" and Merriam Webster's online dictionary defines it as "strong affection for another arising out of kinship or personal ties." White Smoke reports the following, "The word 'love' was once '*leubh', a word used by the Proto-Indo-Europeans approximately five thousand years ago to describe care and desire. When 'love' was incorporated into Old English as 'lufu', it had turned into both a noun to describe, 'deep affection' and its offspring verb, 'to be very fond of'" (Source: WhiteSmoke.com/English Word Series). The earliest chapters of the Bible are believed to have been written 3400 years ago, with most of the Bible being written some 1600 years ago, and of course, Biblical translators did an amazing job at translating the original text. Howbeit, consider this fact—when translating words from one language to another, translators can only use the words that are available in that language; these are the words that are closest to the original text. Was "leubh" the best translation of the love? For that particular language, yes. Let me explain what I mean. The Proto-Indian-Europeans were animistic. Encyclopedia Britannica gave this definition of the word "animism":

> "Belief in innumerable spiritual beings concerned with human affairs and capable of helping or harming human interests. Animistic beliefs were first competently surveyed by Sir Edward Burnett Tylor in his work Primitive Culture (1871), to which is owed the continued currency of the term. While none of the major world religions are animistic (though they may contain animistic elements), most other religions—e.g., those of tribal peoples—are. For this reason, an ethnographic understanding of animism, based on field studies of tribal peoples, is no less important than a theoretical one, concerned with the nature or origin of religion" (Source: Encyclopedia Britannica/Animism).

In short, the Proto-Indidian-Europeans were polytheistic, so their concept of love wasn't exactly biblically based. The word "love" evolved into the Latin word "lubet," which later became "libet" from which we get the word "libido." Later,

it became the Germanic words "lubo, liube, liebe and lob."
It eventually found itself translated into the Old English
"lufu," which means the feeling of love; it also means
affection and sexual attraction. So, am I saying that the
use of the word "love" in the Bible is wrong? Absolutely
not! I'm saying that our understanding of love has been
wrong for thousands of years, and it is for this reason that
we've relegated love to being nothing but a feeling or an
emotion when, in truth:

- Love is a fruit of the Spirit (Galatians 5:22).
- God is Love (1 John 4:8).
- Love never fails (1 Corinthians 13:8).

God is eternal; we know this. He is Alpha (the Beginning)
and Omega (the End); this is why He created the element
of time. Does God have a beginning or an end? No, He is
the Beginning and the End, meaning that all things exist
inside of Him or because of Him. This also means that
nothing can exist outside of Him without His permission.
This includes love. What do I mean by this? It's simple.
There is a human form of love, just as there is a human
version of the truth; we call this a fact. Howbeit, facts can
be proven, just as many of them can be invalidated. This is
evident in the many scientific theories and laws that have
dominated the airways, only to be challenged and
disproved by another scientist just centuries later. The
many advancements in technology can be credited for the
proving and disproving of many of the facts that we once
thought to be truths. But, understand this—a true law is

an immutable fact. If we created, for example, a spectrum with facts on one end and truth on the other end, laws would be in the center of this spectrum. And, by law, I'm not talking about our judicial laws, I'm talking about scientific laws like the law of gravity. What am I saying? Love never fails, which means that it is a truth and a law. Consider these truths:

- Jesus is Truth (John 14:16).
- Jesus is the Word of God (John 1:1, John 1:14).
- The Word will never return to God void (Isaiah 55:11).
- Love never fails (1 Corinthians 13:8).

To get a better understanding of love, consider this—God is eternal and whenever He speaks something into existence, because His Word cannot and will never return to Him void, whatever He speaks can never cease to exist. As we discovered earlier, man's spirit was created before his body. After God created man and woman, He formed the body of a man from the dust of the ground, meaning the body was never spoken into existence, only man's spirit was. This is why the body can die, but the spirit can never cease to exist. Now, there is what the Bible refers to as the "second death," and this is when those who are not written in the Book of Life are tossed into the lake of fire, along with Death and Hell (see Revelation 20:15). What then is hell? It's a holding cell for the dead. Think of it as the waiting room of eternity. It has heights, depths and holding centers. Is there fire in hell? Yes, of course, and we see the evidence of this in the story of the rich man who went to hell. Let's review that story.

- **Luke 16:19-31:** There was a certain rich man, which was clothed in purple and fine linen, and fared sumptuously every day: And there was a certain beggar named Lazarus, which was laid at his gate, full of sores, and desiring to be fed with the crumbs which fell from the rich man's table: moreover the dogs came and licked his sores. And it came to pass, that the beggar died, and was carried by the angels into Abraham's bosom: the rich man also died, and was buried; and in hell he lift up his eyes, being in torments, and seeth Abraham afar off, and Lazarus in his bosom. And he cried and said, Father Abraham, have mercy on me, and send Lazarus, that he may dip the tip of his finger in water, and cool my tongue; for I am tormented in this flame. But Abraham said, Son, remember that thou in thy lifetime receivedst thy good things, and likewise Lazarus evil things: but now he is comforted, and thou art tormented. And beside all this, between us and you there is a great gulf fixed: so that they which would pass from hence to you cannot; neither can they pass to us, that would come from thence. Then he said, I pray thee therefore, father, that thou wouldest send him to my father's house: For I have five brethren; that he may testify unto them, lest they also come into this place of torment. Abraham saith unto him, They have Moses and the prophets; let them hear them. And he said,

Nay, father Abraham: but if one went unto them
from the dead, they will repent. And he said unto
him, If they hear not Moses and the prophets,
neither will they be persuaded, though one rose
from the dead.

But wait! What then are the dead? When a person's body
ceases to function, the spirit or eternal part of that person
can no longer walk the Earth because our bodies are our
Earth suits; they are what legalize our existence in the
Earth. Therefore, our spirits have to go somewhere. If we
are not saved, our spirits cannot exist in God's Kingdom.
Keep in mind that hell was created for Satan and his angels
(see Matthew 25:41), and when God judged the angels
who'd betrayed and fallen away from Him, He'd cast them
out of Heaven, meaning, He'd removed them from His
presence. God is light (see 1 John 1:5), so outside of God's
presence is darkness. This means that Satan and his angels
went on to exist outside of God. God then created the
Heaven and the Earth, and when He created the Earth, the
Bible tells us that darkness (or the dwelling place of devils)
was upon the face of the deep. Believe it or not, this
darkness is what we now refer to as outer space. Outer
space is one of the three Heavens (see the chart below).

Heavens	Location	Scripture
Third Heaven	God's Throne Room	2 Corinthians 12:2
Second Heaven	Celestial Heaven; Outer Space	Matthew 24:29

First Heaven	Atmospheric Heaven	Genesis 1:6-8

The first Heaven is the atmosphere that surrounds the Earth. It extends to about twenty miles above the Earth. The second Heaven is what we refer to as outer space; this space includes the sun, moon, the stars and the other planets. And finally, there is the third Heaven. This is the throne room of God. King Solomon wrote in 1 Kings 8:27, "But will God indeed dwell on the earth? Behold, heaven and the heaven of heavens cannot contain You. How much less this temple which I have built!" There are so many mysteries that have yet to be revealed, but let's look at Revelation 12:3-4 once again; it reads, "And there appeared another wonder in heaven; and behold a great red dragon, having seven heads and ten horns, and seven crowns upon his heads. And his tail drew the third part of the stars of heaven, and did cast them to the earth: and the dragon stood before the woman which was ready to be delivered, for to devour her child as soon as it was born." As mentioned in Relational Acuity 1.0, the stars mentioned here are angels; these were the third of the angels that Satan managed to deceive and build his army with. They are what we now refer to as demons or devils. And get this—they can never cease to exist! Why is this? Because they are spirits and spirits are words of God, but because they can no longer exist in His presence, God created a container for them; this is what we call hell. People often ask, "If God is a God of love, why would He cast people in hell?" The quick answer to this question is—His Word cannot return to Him void. Why? Because it is impossible for Him to lie (see Hebrews 6:18), plus, He is Truth. So, when God judged fallen spirits, mankind automatically fell under the same judgment once he sinned. But because God is love and He loves us, He sent His Son, Christ Jesus, to redeem us. Howbeit, hell is the trashcan of spirituality. Because spirits are eternal and evil spirits cannot walk with God (see Amos 3:3), God had to create a space for them. That space is hell. And again, hell will be tossed into the lake of fire; this is an eternal lake of fire, and when the Bible says that the smoke of their torment will rise forever, we have to understand that we exist in time, but time exists in God. However, God is timeless, meaning He is eternal. And just like God is eternal, spirits are eternal; this includes us, after all, we are spirits living in bodies. So, when we step outside of time, we will step into eternity. What does all of this have to do with love? It's simple—God is love, therefore, love is eternal. It is also one of the fruits of the Spirit.

Galatians 5:22-23 reads, "But the fruit of the Spirit is love, joy, peace, longsuffering, gentleness, goodness, faith, meekness, temperance: against such there is no law." Believe it or not, none of these are emotions; they are the fruits of the Kingdom. Think of it this way—Adam and Eve once lived in the Garden of Eden, and in that Garden were many trees that they could eat from. Again, gardens are places of order. Therefore, the fruits of the

Spirit are the embodiment of God's character that He gives us to consume so that we can be more like Him. All the same, they allow us to grow our character in the midst of adversity. You see, once we pick up the character of God, we then pick up His characteristics; these are the fruits of the Spirit. The objective is to get these expressions into our conscious minds through the reading and studying of God's Word, and then ultimately, get them into our hearts. But, wait! This isn't the final stop since these are fruits of the Spirit! God wants us to practice these traits until they enter into our subconscious minds and become habits! Another word for "habit" is "stronghold." This means that God will build a fortress around our hearts; He will be our Strong Tower. This also means that we'll learn to love from the heart, and not just our intellect. Note: intellectual love is what we talked about earlier; it's the world's definition and expression of what they believe love to be, which is why it repeatedly fails.

Now, let's come to understand how to cultivate Kingdom relationships. As a reminder—since God is love, please understand that when someone says "I love you," that person is literally saying, "I have God's heart for you." Here's the truth—if the person doesn't have God's heart, how can he or she have God's heart for you? They can't! In layman's terms, the individual is offering you something that is wrapped in conditions and time, but God's love is both unconditional and timeless. The closest expression we see to Agape (unconditional love) is the love that a mother has for her children (in most cases). Regardless of what her children do, most mothers will repeatedly forgive them, even if the world hates them. She will shield them with her life, and she will never leave them (even though they can leave her). The same is true for some fathers, of course, but we see this measure of love mostly materializing through mothers. This is to say that we don't find this level, measure or mastery of love in most romantic relationships. As a matter of fact, a large majority of men have this measure of love for their male friends, but again, in the romance arena, relationships that are built in the spectrum of agape love are relatively rare and they continue to diminish because we have been taught and we are teaching our kids that love is an emotion. Consequently, we have an entire generation of people who are emotionally immature and unstable. To get a better understanding of love so that we can build Kingdom relationships, let's look at Matthew 22:37-40, which reads, "Jesus said unto him, Thou shalt love the Lord thy God with all thy heart, and with all thy soul, and with all thy mind. This is the first and great commandment. And the second is like unto it, Thou shalt love thy neighbor as thyself. On these two commandments hang all the law and the prophets." Matthew 6:33 reads, "But seek ye first the kingdom of God, and his righteousness; and all these things shall be added unto you." The keyword in both of these scriptures is "first." Whatever we give God first, He sanctifies and multiplies. And this is why love is declining in the Earth today. Instead, we see the continual rising of self-love (selfishness), and while self-love is needed and necessary, it is toxic if it has not been sanctified by God and paired with brotherly love. Again, the only way it can be sanctified is if we love God first. Think of God as a prism of light, but the light that we see emanating through Him is love. When we take our small measures of love and give them to Him first, He removes the world's residue and the conditions from it; this process is called purification. Note: there is no purification without santification. He then multiplies it and shines it back to us and through us. This causes the glory of God to radiate from us even more. And, get this—demons can see this love; to them, it looks like light. This is why witches and people who embrace demonic doctrines report seeing what they call "auras" around people. This light both attracts people to us and repels people from us. Now, you can understand why some people hate you without a cause; you can understand why some people (yes, people who even profess to be believers) have shunned you. Understand that they are not rejecting you, they are rejecting the God in you. So, one of the first practices that you'll have to master if you want to build Kingdom relationships is loving God with all that you are and all that you have. This is the process of sanctification. This is the moment when you allow God to, for example, take you off the dating market, pause or end some of your friendships and place a standard or boundary between you and some (or most) of your relatives. Of course, this is not how that process looks for everyone; this is just an example. During this phase, your objective is to focus on God; that's it and that's all. You are to pursue Him through study, prayer and practice. And, by practice, I mean that your job is to reproduce His fruits in the Earth, even when you don't understand or agree with them. This means that you have to allow the Word to enter your conscious, and then your heart. From there, your assignment is to let the Word dig through the 30-fold dimension until it reaches the 60-fold dimension. After this, you have to allow God's Word to reach the 100-fold dimension of your heart until it plows through your subconscious and enters your unconscious dimension. But remember, we're still in the 60-fold dimension; this is the soul. Again, humans are comprised of a body, soul and spirit. The ultimate objective is to allow your spirit to marry itself to God's Spirit, and by marry, I mean to come into agreement with God's Word. Of course, most people will never reach this dimension, which is why the majority of people on the Earth will never know what it's like to be truly loved by a romantic partner. The same is true for platonic relationships (unless both parties are male). Why do (most) male friendships survive the tests of time? The Bible refers to women as the weaker vessels; this isn't just a reference to a woman's natural strength, it is a reference to mental and emotional strength. Simply put, there are degrees of emotionalism, and the more emotionally sensitive you are, the weaker you are emotionally. This is why the fathers in the biblical days were the first points of contact that a man had if he was interested in a woman. They could not date a woman back then; the men had to observe them from a distance, consider the integrity of the women's fathers and then decide if they wanted to intermarry into those families. A man's name was incredibly important back then. This is why a man with a powerful or great name could request a much higher bride price than the average man, and the bride price was not a transaction. Most families were industrial back then, and a man's children worked with him in whatever trade he worked in. So, when a man married off his daughter, he would be losing that extra hand, and therefore losing wages. The goal of the bride price was to replace what he would lose and to prove, not just the integrity of the potential groom, but to prove and demonstrate his ability to provide for his bride-to-be. So, if a man was interested in a woman, he could not express his interest to her (this would be considered manipulation since women are sensitive). This is the equivalent of what the western world does to children. Children are emotionally underdeveloped. All the same, sugar is addictive. So, in most of our supermarkets, you'll notice that when you're standing in line at the register, there is a wall of candy to your right or left (sometimes both). The objective here is to appeal to your sweet tooth, of course, but it's mostly to appeal to your children since they are emotionally unstable. This is why children can shop with their parents for hours on end, and then lose their cool at the register. Men are like candy to (most) women, and this is why Satan worked tirelessly to remove the head (fathers) from most families. This is like removing the parents at the checkouts, allowing a child to run loose at the registers, and then sending the bill to the parents once the toddler is done ripping through every package that he or she can reach (this includes the child's medical bills from the tummy ache that followed the child's rampage). I'm saying this to say that Satan is strategic; he skillfully removed the father-figure from many homes; this in itself, broke a lot of women, and then he left the window open for a lot of broken men to enter. The key here is brokenness. Most people want to build relationships on top of their own brokenness. Of course, Satan's main goal has been to disconnect us from God; this way, he can rule over us. He has attempted this by causing us to believe that love is an emotion, and then creating movies and music to promote this ideology. There are emotional aspects of love, but love itself is eternal and unconditional.

The good news is that there are people on Earth who've followed the Word and found love, and by this, I mean that they're overflowing with God's love. These people are the lights of the world; they are the ones who have chosen to allow God to operate in and through them. And because they are little lights, God hides them; this doesn't mean that He places them in hidden caves somewhere out in the wilderness. It simply means that they look like everyday people. This is why Proverbs 18:22 (NIV) states, "He who finds a wife finds a good thing and obtains favor from the LORD." All the same, not every married man has favor; we know this. We've seen men married to some really broken and toxic women. Therefore, by "wife," God isn't necessarily talking about two people getting married, He's talking about a man being wise enough to distinguish a wife (someone He's hidden) from a woman (someone who reveals or uncovers herself). I often tell people this—if you marry a woman, she won't become a wife (by God's definition of that word); instead, she'll become a married woman. The same is true on the other end of the spectrum. If you marry a man, he won't become a husband (by God's definition of a husband), he'll become a married man.

The point is—you have to love God first, and then become a living embodiment of His love. By doing this and remaining in His will, He will bring the right relationships to you, be they platonic, professional or romantic. He will even help you to properly categorize your familial relationships, along with your other relationships. Relational categorization is necessary to maintain, not just peace, but longevity. Most people are far behind on their life's journeys because they've spent too much time learning lessons that many of them have yet to grasp. Unfortunately, a great number of people spend the entirety of their lives searching for love outside of God, not realizing that the voids that they have can only be satisfied by the Most High Love (YAHWEH). And again, when we follow our own personal instruction manual (the Bible) and we seek the Kingdom of God first, according to the scriptures, God will give us everything else (see

Matthew 6:33). This includes the desires of our hearts, after (of course) He's given us a new heart and a new mind. To grow your relational acuity, you have to take time out to date, court and ultimately marry God. And by marrying God, I don't mean that you need to host a ceremony or loudly proclaim a set of well-written vows at God; in short, you have to come into agreement with God. This means you have to:

1. **Get knowledge.** You do this by studying and showing yourself approved (30-Fold).
2. **Get understanding.** You do this by chewing or ruminating the knowledge that you've acquired. In short, you have to do a deep-dive into the many principles that the Bible introduces us to. This means that you have to find people who are smarter than you are, and glean from them.
3. **Get wisdom.** You do this by applying what you know and understand. By repeatedly studying and plowing for the truth, God will grant you access to wisdom (supernatural, divine knowledge and understanding).

30-Fold	60-Fold	100-Fold
Knowledge	Understanding	Wisdom
Conscious	Subconscious	Unconscious

The chart above gives you an understanding of how information roots itself. Once it reaches the heart, your transformation begins. And once you become wise, please note that you'll become rare. Contrary to popular belief, being rare is not always fun; it can be lonely and, at the same time, you have to master fighting rejection because what you'll soon discover is that you have a greater (and more mature) love than most people. This could ultimately result in you finding yourself in a lot of one-sided relationships where you are genuinely and healthily loving another human being who has little to no ability to love you in return. This is why you have to chase God and allow Him to bring the right people into your life and remember to test the spirits in the people, not just to see whether or not they need deliverance (most people need deliverance from something), but to see whether or not you should place them in your intellectual circle or your intimate circle. The right placement of people not only fuels your destiny, but it helps you to enjoy the ride there. The misplacement or wrong placement of people sets the stage for confusion and trauma, both of which delay your destiny. With confusion, you spend too much of the time allotted to you chasing a reality (realm) that God never called you to, and this causes you to go in circles. Another word for "circles" here is "cycles." You'll find yourself repeating some of the same behaviors over and over again, hoping to get a different result, which is the very definition of insanity. Trauma, on the other hand, increases the size of your voids, thus creating an even greater hunger (this materializes as desperation) and a greater gravitational pull of attraction, meaning, you'll find yourself attracted to people you ordinarily would avoid. It also delays your destiny because you have to spend too much time healing. And most people don't fully heal; they just use other people as bandages. But, if you follow God wholeheartedly, He will do as He's promised to do, and that is—give you the desires of your heart. He will also use you as an example so that others can be motivated to seek Him.

So, what is the Kingdom's love-code? It's first. The code to favor, love, blessings and sanity is f-i-r-s-t. Simply put, you have to pursue, find and embrace the heart of God first so that you can become an even greater light of God in the Earth. You have to forsake all other relationships that draw you away or distract you from God, and allow Him to change your life by changing your mind. Remember, He does this through the use of information. Keep God first and you will never fail; keep God first and you will never feel the sting of humiliation again! You have to give Him a higher rank in your life than you give to yourself and/or others. And lastly, please know that this particular process isn't always easy, especially since the flesh and the spirit are contrary or at odds with one another. It can be both frustrating and rewarding because on one hand, you'll see the positive changes being made to your life. All the same, you'll notice that your phone isn't ringing as much as it used to, your friends may begin to fall away and your family may even start to mock and ridicule you, but don't allow these events to dissuade you. Instead, let them encourage you, knowing that what God has for you is far greater than what you had in store for yourself.

Don't just grow your relational acuity, put everything you've learned into practice, and do this religiously until it becomes a law in your life. When your relational acuity matures, you will notice just how different your world looks and how lighter the air appears to be in that particular world. When this happens, you'll be so overwhelmingly blessed by the results that you'll encourage others to take this journey as well! Let me be the first to welcome you to your next level of relational acuity!

TIERED RELATIONSHIPS

In the previous chapter, we talked about familiarity and protocol, and in this chapter, we are going to talk about building tiered relationships. But before we delve into this topic, let's revisit the topic of honor versus dishonor. Growing up, my parents required us to use the terms "ma'am" and "sir" when speaking to adults. All the same, they demonstrated this by always referencing people older than themselves as "ma'am" and "sir." They also referenced authority figures in the same manner. I remember that the majority of the time I heard my mother talking on the phone, I would hear her using these terms of endearment. And I've never heard her refer to her mother or father by their first names; I've never heard my mother say "huh" or "what" to them or any authority figure for that matter. This means that she didn't just make us honor our elders and those in positions of authority, she demonstrated it. The same was true for my dad. So, honor isn't just something I do; it's embedded in my DNA. It's not my culture, it's now a part of my character. Even when my mother was on her deathbed, I remember listening to her refer to her doctor as "ma'am," even though she was sometimes incoherent. Whenever the nurses came to visit her in hospice, regardless of their ages, she would refer to them as "ma'am" or "sir," and for this reason, I truly love and appreciate her. This is because she left me with one of the greatest gifts (outside of

Christ), and that is the gift of honor. She never explained honor to me. In truth, I don't think she even understood it. Nevertheless, she demonstrated it to me time and time again, so I didn't have to understand why honor was important. I just knew it was important. Romans 13:7 says, "Render therefore to all their dues: tribute to whom tribute is due; custom to whom custom; fear to whom fear; honour to whom honor." All the same, I have truly witnessed what dishonor and disrespect does to the mind of a person. It sets the stage for entitlement and extreme narcissism; I've also noticed what appears to be a link between dishonor and some mental disorders. People who repeatedly dishonor others tend to be emotionally unstable, fearful, distrustful, paranoid, confrontational and oftentimes even hateful. The reason for this is because dishonor closes doors that they feel entitled to. Consequently, many people who've never learned to honor others end up with a victim's mentality; this isn't just a mentality, it is a disease of the mind. They always feel like someone has wronged them, people are jealous of them or someone has spoken reproachfully about them, causing some opportunities to be snatched from under them. I've come in contact with my fair share of entitled people, and I'll be honest with you—I've found that there is literally no satisfying them, outside of allowing them to control you or get whatever it is that they want, regardless of who or what it may affect. The truth is—dishonor is the doorway to curses.

What is a tiered relationship? Let's look at a couple of scriptures:

- **Ephesians 5:23**: For the husband is the head of the wife, even as Christ is the head of the church: and he is the saviour of the body. Therefore as the church is subject unto Christ, so let the wives be to their own husbands in every thing.
- **1 Corinthians 11:3**: But I would have you know, that the head of every man is Christ; and the head of the woman is the man; and the head of Christ is God.
- **1 Peter 5:5 (ESV)**: Likewise, you who are younger, be subject to the elders. Clothe yourselves, all of you, with humility toward one another, for "God opposes the proud but gives grace to the humble.

To understand a tiered relationship, think about Abraham and Sarah's relationship in the Bible. According to the aforementioned scriptures, the husband is the head or highest-ranking person in a household. In truth, it's almost scary to preach this today because a lot of women have either experienced abuse from men in authority or they've watched their mothers be abused. Then again, some women never experienced abuse; they were just taught that men and women are equal, and while this is true, equal in value does not equate to equal in rank ... not, at least, in God's eyes. After all, He created the concept of rank. In Genesis 3:16, God went on record with these words as He spoke to Eve; He said, "Unto the woman he said, I will greatly multiply thy sorrow and thy conception; in sorrow thou shalt bring forth children; and thy desire shall be to thy husband, and he shall rule over thee." While this was the result of the fall of mankind, get this, it was not a part of the punishment! Before the fall, there was no need for rank in human relationships because, for one, they were not yet humans or humbled, and two, the couple was blameless or sinless. This means that they were not yet a part of the war between good and evil. As a matter of fact, they weren't even aware of this war. They were innocent; they were pure. Howbeit, when they fell into sin, God had to institute a system of order similar to the one in the Kingdom so that Satan wouldn't divide the family unit by causing both parties and/or their children to war for the position of power. A two-headed creature is not a healthy one, meaning, there couldn't be two heads of one house. Just like Jesus is the head of the church, we are the body or members. This is also why Lucifer's attempt to be like God or to rule alongside Him would never and could never take place. And sadly enough, when the concept of submission is taught, it has to be an entire lesson or series because of the hurt some women have endured at the hands of their fathers and their partners/spouses. Therefore, when talking about headship, leadership and submission, a leader often has to go into detail because some of the women seated in the congregation or in the online audience immediately start thinking about the men in their lives or the men who were once a part of their lives, so rather than hearing that there are men who are healthy and Godly enough to be submitted to, all these women hear is the leader saying that they should submit to men like the ones who've hurt them. Consequently, they have what is called a trauma response. The following information was taken from MindBodyGreen:

> "A trauma response is the reflexive use of over-adaptive coping mechanisms in the real or perceived presence of a trauma event, according to trauma therapist Cynthia M.A. Siadat, LCSW. The four trauma responses most commonly recognized are fight, flight, freeze, fawn, sometimes called the 4 Fs of trauma" (Source: www.mindbodygreen.com/Fight, Flight, Freeze, Fawn: Examining The 4 Trauma Responses/Julie Nguyen).

Quick Note for Single Women

Why did I share the aforementioned information? This is to say that if you find yourself feeling angry, scared or triggered at the concept of submission, please consider your past. Has anyone ever truly protected you? Has any man ever truly provided for you? Have you ever felt safe in a relationship? Have you ever truly experienced love from a man? If not, it is normal for you to feel upset or offended whenever the topic of men heading the household is brought up, but keep in mind that the Bible isn't telling you to submit to an ungodly man or the men from your past; God is simply telling you to heal and grow until you reach the height (mentally, emotionally and spiritually) of a God-fearing man; this way, you can experience both safety and love in a husband/wife relationship. However, if you keep dating men on a particular level, it goes without saying that it will be nearly impossible to submit to them, given the fact that they aren't submitted to God, nor are they submitted to any Godly authorities.

One of the reasons the concept of having tiered relationships or submitting to authority figures is so offensive today to many people is because they've been abused by authority figures. All the same, when talking about the concept of submission, most people don't truly understand submission; they genuinely think that the Bible is telling people to let other people control them, and this is NOT what submission means. Submission is a product of trust, but get this—we will always submit to:

1. The truth about a person.
2. What we think is the truth about that person.

For example, Dianna is married to a man named Dean. The couple identify themselves as Christians and they have been married for more than eight years. One day, Dean calls his wife and says, "Hey, I'm going out to dinner with my co-workers when I get off. I'll be home around nine tonight." Dianna immediately hangs up the phone and throws it across the room, where it hits the wall and then lands on her bed. Miraculously, the phone doesn't shatter. Four minutes later, Dean calls Dianna again; she doesn't answer her phone. He calls back three times before she answers. "What is wrong with you now?!" he shouts. "Am I not allowed to have dinner with my co-workers?! Dianna, I'm getting really tired of this!" Dianna thinks about hanging up the phone again, but instead, she pauses before answering. "Do you think I was born yesterday?" she asks sarcastically. "You think I don't know what your plans are?! Dean, you are as predictable as you are stupid! Have fun! I'll be waiting for you when you get home!" With those words, Dianna hangs up the phone again, and then powers it down so that her husband cannot call her back. She then walks over to her computer and starts watching one of her favorite shows on YouTube. Her computer chimes, indicating that she's gotten an email. Knowing that it's her husband emailing her from his office computer, Dianna ignores the email and keeps looking for the latest episode of her favorite show. Two hours pass, and at 5:25, Dianna hears her living room door opening and closing. Every negative emotion begins to flood her thoughts. Dean walks into the couple's bedroom where Dianna is sitting at the computer, opens the closet, and then proceeds to grab a suitcase. Dianna hears the sound of the suitcase's zipper, but she ignores her husband as she continues to watch her computer screen. He angrily packs his bags while mumbling under his breath. And then, his anger reaches an all-time high when he attempts to pull down a few of his jeans from the top of the closet, causing an avalanche of clothes and shoes to fall, some of which hit his face before he manages to turn his head. This causes Dean's nose to start bleeding. Filled with rage, Dean begins to swear loudly.

"This is what happens when you marry the most insecure woman alive!" he shouts as he wipes his nose with his shirt. "Dianna, I want a divorce!" Dianna stands up and walks out of the room, completely ignoring her husband. She walks into the living room, takes the huge picture of her and her husband off the wall, and then smashes it on the floor. "Get out of my house!" she shouts. Hearing the sounds of glass shattering and his wife screaming, Dean emerges with fury in his eyes and blood on his shirt. "Dianna," he says calmly. "I think ... I think ... I think you need some serious help; I think I made a mistake coming back here. I'll take what I packed and I never want to see you again." Is Dianna insecure? Maybe. Then again, Dianna is submissive, but she's submissive to the truth regarding her husband or, at minimum, her perception of her husband's intentions. Let me explain. Dean has had a history of committing adultery, and one pattern Dean had when he was doing so was going out to lunch with his co-workers. However, Dean got off at five o'clock in the evening; those dinner dates would often end around 7:30, and Dean would almost always come around at 11:00. He'd promised to never do this again, but it appeared that this behavior was starting to resurface. Does this justify Dianna's behavior? Absolutely not, but it does explain it. Believe it or not, Dianna's reaction to Dean's desire to hang out with his co-workers is a trauma response. The four types of trauma responses are fight, flight, fawn or freeze. The following information was taken from MBG Health:

"**Fight:** When healthy, the fight response can allow

for assertion and solid boundaries. When unhealthy—
i.e., when used as a trauma response—it's an active
self-preservation function where you move
reactively toward conflict with anger and
aggression. It's a fear state where you confront the
threat to stand up and assert yourself.

Flight: When faced with a dangerous situation, the
flight response corresponds with avoidant behavior.
When you're healthy, you're able to be discerning in
stressful situations and disengage within limits.
However, as a trauma response, you take it a step
further by isolating yourself entirely.

Freeze: When healthy, the freeze response can help
you slow down and appraise the situation carefully
to determine the next steps. When unhealthy, the
freeze response relates to dissociation and
immobilizing behaviors. When this defense is
enacted, it often results in literally "freezing"—
feeling frozen and unable to move or finding
yourself spacing out as if you're in a haze or
detached from reality. You don't feel like you're
really there, and you're mentally checked out as you
leave out what's happening in your surroundings and
what you're feeling in an attempt to find emotional
safety.

Fawn: At its core, fawning is about people-pleasing
and engaging in pacifying behaviors. It's
characterized by prioritizing people above all else by
doing whatever they want to diffuse conflict and

receive their approval. It seems good to be well liked and defer to others to secure safety, but not when it's at the cost of losing yourself. It can reach a point where you abandon yourself and your needs by merging so thoroughly with others. Most likely, you don't feel seen by others and may feel eclipsed by the people in your life" (Source: www.mindbodygreen.com/Fight, Flight, Freeze, Fawn: Examining The 4 Trauma Responses/Julie Nguyen).

In truth, a lot of marriages are destroyed by trauma responses. Some of those trauma responses are the results of events that took place before the couple even met, while others occurred in the marriage. Either way, when trauma is not properly addressed by both parties, the results can be both painful and permanent. Note: if you've experienced trauma and you've noticed that you tend to overreact whenever you're hurt, scared or offended, it would be wise for you to find a good, Godly therapist (not your pastor) so you can start your healing journey. Again, many marriages and relationships are destroyed by trauma responses. Also note that if adultery took place in a marriage, it can be incredibly traumatic to the spouse who was cheated on. This means that if the marriage is going to survive the event, both parties have to be all-in as it relates to doing what it takes to heal. The offending spouse has to be especially sensitive to the other spouse's pain. The following information was taken from Choosing Therapy:

> "Infidelity can be traumatic, causing intensely painful emotions for the person who was cheated on. They may actually experience symptoms of post-traumatic stress disorder (PTSD), including heightened anxiety, intrusive thoughts, and emotional distress. Ultimately, the level of distress one can experience depends on their unique situation as well as how they internalize and cope with the infidelity" (Source: Choosing Therapy/Infidelity PTSD: Symptoms & How to Cope/Jaclyn Gulotta).

Understanding this, you can now sympathize with Dianna. All the same, you may sympathize with Dean. Either way, both Dean and Dianna need therapy.

And again, submission has everything to do with a truth or perception. What if I told you that we all naturally submit to what we believe? Dean had a habit of cheating; this is the truth that his wife was submitted to. Dianna had trouble controlling her temper; this is the truth her husband was submitted to. Arguments are oftentimes the product of pride and a lack of self-reflection. In other words, disagreements tend to arise when there is a lack of accountability and an abundance of hypocrisy. Dean needed to become trustworthy; he needed to give her a foundation to rebuild her trust on. This foundation is always built on history and habits, not words. Dianna needed to work towards healing so that she could fully forgive her husband. Neither of these are easy feats to accomplish, especially given the fact that most humans are impatient. God often tosses couples at me when they've tried everything and they are on the verge of filing for divorce. I don't like counseling married couples because of my marital history, but in truth, that's what qualifies me for the most complex cases (even though I always do one or two sessions before referring them to someone else). What I've witnessed repeatedly is this—one person has a bad habit or pattern, but he or she wants the other person to submit to a truth that doesn't exist. Dean and Dianna's case is a perfect example. Dean wanted his wife to trust him, even though he's repeatedly proven himself to be untrustworthy. Because of this, she trusted his history and not his words. It is both asinine and unrealistic to demand a spouse that has been betrayed to completely ignore your history with him or her if you haven't given that person something to trust in, after all, trust has to be built. It can never be forced or pulled out of thin air. I'm not saying this because it sounds good, I'm saying this because I've counseled enough couples to see how this particular dynamic plays out. After a traumatic event, couples need to immediately immerse themselves in pastoral, marital and individual counseling. Marital counseling alone typically won't fix the problems, and while I do highly recommend marital counseling, it more so deals with the fruit of the issues, and not the root of the issues. Pastoral and deliverance counseling deals with the spiritual side of the issue, but individual counseling deals with the practical side of it all. Individual counseling would help Dean to understand why he chose to have an affair in the first place. Every branch of counseling is needed, but all too often, couples ignore individual counseling in favor of marital counseling. Marital counseling teaches the spouse how to behave in a marriage, all the while, suppressing those evil desires that have been brought on by, for example, childhood traumas, unforgiveness, rejection, addictions (porn, alcohol, drugs, attention, etc.). Don't get me wrong—marital counseling is both invaluable and needed, but never forsake individual counseling. Thankfully, there are Christian leaders who offer a combo of individual, marital and pastoral/deliverance counseling. One such leader is Apostle Ivory Hopkins, along with his beautiful wife, Elder Evelyn Hopkins. The point of this is—whenever you find yourself in a position of leadership, remember this—people will always believe and submit to what they see and not necessarily what you say; that is if what you say doesn't align with what they see. This is true in marriages, professional relationships and every relational category. Then again, people with a history of traumas tend to submit to their perceptions, insecurities and traumas; that is, of course, if they don't get the healing they need to let go of the pain, fear and beliefs brought on by those events. This is why it is imperative that we heal before we start building intimate relationships with people, after all, an intimate relationship (simply put) is someone granting you access to his or her heart. If your heart is broken, you will intentionally or unintentionally break that person's heart because we instinctively reproduce in others what has been produced or reproduced in us.

Below are a few benefits of tiered relationships.

1. They create order, whereas, non-tiered relationships create either chaos, disorder or a perversion of God's original design of a thing. Perversion opens the door for performance, all the while, slamming the door on love and its benefits, and wherever you see performance, you will eventually witness or experience a burnout.
2. They compel God to bless the relationship because order is a Kingdom concept.
3. They produce true partnerships where the roles aren't confused; this prevents competition, division and unrealistic expectations.
4. They produce true leaders, after all, leaders ascend, and as they do this, they make their fair share of mistakes and they grow and learn from those mistakes. They then teach others to ascend and avoid those same issues.
5. They produce compassionate leaders because compassion is a product of empathy, and empathy is more powerful when it's fueled by experience.
6. They give us someone to model ourselves after.
7. They help to give us language to the seasons and experiences we will someday face. When a leader

goes before you, that leader can help you to better understand the varying pressures that you will experience on your journey, and believe it or not, this alone is powerful enough to prevent a massive number of suicides and suicide attempts. This is why the Bible says there is safety in the multitude of counselors (see Proverbs 11:4).

8. They break demonic and destructive cycles and thought patterns. For example, let's say that your father had a habit of gambling every time he got his paycheck. This set the stage for problems in his marriage to your mother and the two wives he had thereafter. As an adult, you've never witnessed a man making an earnest living, so you find yourself looking for quick ways to make money. Howbeit, you join a mentorship program where you're mentored by a man who's not only a hard worker, but he's also a smart worker. He teaches you discipline and helps you to discover the ingenuity behind your gifting; this is the same gifting that your father had, but it had been perverted. So, he teaches you that you're great at repetition; this is usually the crux behind addiction. This repetitiveness causes you to be dedicated whenever you're inventing things and building systems because you won't give up anytime something fails; instead, you'll discover where you went wrong and go at it again.

9. There's someone around to inspect and correct you.

A lot of people don't know this, but we actually flourish when we receive instruction and correction. People who hate correction usually end up being the smartest people in their circles, and this is dangerous! It sets the stage for pride, and pride ushers in the spirit of destruction. "Pride goes before destruction, and a haughty spirit before a fall" (Proverbs 6:18).

10. You learn to master honor; this removes the limitations from your potential.

Tiered relationships are very similar to steps or stairs, while non-tiered relationships are like slopes; they're slippery, unstable and require more energy to ascend. In tiered relationships, each role is clearly defined (when communicated), whereas in non-tiered relationships, roles are more fluid and undefined. This opens the door for ungodly ambition, competition, instability, insecurity and chaos. "Where there is no guidance, a people falls, but in an abundance of counselors there is safety" (Proverbs 11:14). Think about a relationship between parents and their children. For example, Amanda is a single mother of two girls, ages four and seven. Her oldest daughter, Rachel, is relatively docile, while her youngest daughter, Hannah, is somewhat assertive and demanding. Because of this, Hannah tends to bully Rachel. And Amanda is not too big on discipline; she doesn't take away any of Hannah's toys whenever she misbehaves, nor does she take away any of her privileges. She simply yells at her daughter. Because of this, Hannah slowly begins to bully her mother. It started with her throwing tantrums and breaking things at home, and it has grown into full-blown rebellion, whereas Rachel now throws objects at her mother, she's been expelled from two schools and she can scream and cry for hours whenever she doesn't get her way. Will this behavior "cure" itself? Not at all. In tiered relationships, the person in authority has the primary responsibility of:

1. **Being the Architect:** Creating a blueprint of what he or she is building. For example, the Bible refers to the wife as the help meet; this means that a man should be in his purpose and building whatever God gave him to build before he finds a wife. In other words, he must know what he needs help with, otherwise, his help meet won't know what to assist him with.

2. **Being the Lawmaker:** This means that the individual must set guidelines; these are the rules, limitations and boundaries that govern whatever it is that he or she is building. This is why Joshua said, "And if it seem evil unto you to serve the LORD, choose you this day whom ye will serve; whether the gods which your fathers served that were on the other side of the flood, or the gods of the Amorites, in whose land ye dwell: but as for me and my house, we will serve the LORD" (Joshua 24:15). And by house, he meant the members of his household. In other words, Joshua was saying what was legal and illegal in his home. As the husband, he was the

strongman of his home. "No man can enter into a strong man's house, and spoil his goods, except he will first bind the strong man; and then he will spoil his house" (Mark 3:27).

3. **Being the Governor:** This means that he or she needs something to govern. Going back to the husband/wife example, if a man lives with his parents and brings his new bride into his parents' home, he is not the head of that home; his father and/or mother is.

4. **Being the Enforcer:** This is the officer of the law; this is the one who executes the laws, rules and guidelines that have been established. And so that this is not taken out of context, a great example is, a husband may say to his wife, "Because we are trying to buy a house, please abide by a $100 beauty budget for the next two months, and let's see about scaling it back $10 a month thereafter. We don't need to do any reckless spending." If the wife agrees but does not abide by the beauty budget, he has to enforce the guidelines by placing a withdrawal limit on their bank account, whereas they both need one another's consent to withdraw a certain amount of money.

5. **Being the Example:** In a marriage, both parties set guidelines, but the husband has to lead by example; this is what allows his wife to trust his lead, and again, people submit naturally where trust is established.

Also, let's establish this fact—some tiered relationships are platonic. All of your friends have been granted a measure of rank in the realm of the spirit. So, if you're a mature Christian who has managed to sacrifice your flesh, grow in the things of God, discipline yourself and reap the fruits of your good and Godly choices, please understand that you are rare. This would mean that you may outrank (in maturity) many of your Christian friends. If you notice that you're wiser than one of your friends, for example, and you're always having to pour wisdom into her, help her when she's feeling down and pay for most of the meals whenever the two of you go out, she's not your friend; she's your mentee. And if you don't place the right label on this relationship, you will end up hurt and offended. This is a tiered relationships, meaning you are the head or leader in that dynamic. Don't get me wrong—in a relative relationship, meaning the two of you are eye-to-eye in rank, you will have seasons where you're pouring out more than your friend is, and there will be seasons when he or she is pouring more into you than you're pouring in him or her. I call this the Seesaw Effect. What is the Seesaw Effect? It's when a relationship repeatedly shifts. A great example of this is an event that took place when I was in my early twenties. I worked in retail, and I had several friendship branches in that store, and by branches, I mean that some of my friends didn't affiliate or associate themselves with one another, so I had a separate relationship with all of them. I used to go to lunch with one of those friends regularly. One day, I asked her if she was ready to go to lunch. She told me that she didn't have any money, so she'd sit it out. "I got you," I said, meaning I would pay for the meal. I could tell she wasn't all-too-comfortable with the idea of me paying for her food, but she came along anyway. The next day, the same thing happened. I asked her if she was ready for lunch, and she reminded me that she didn't have any money. Once again, I insisted on paying for the meal. This continued for the entirety of that week. The next week, she walked up to me and excitedly told me about a surprise check she'd received in the mail. It was from back child support. I rejoiced with her, but I'd spent all of my money the week prior. Around noon, she asked me if I was ready to go to lunch. I told her that I was broke, and to my surprise, she said, "Okay," and then left. She went and got herself something to eat and did not offer to buy me anything. I was taken aback. I couldn't believe what I was witnessing. So, for the rest of that week, I watched her go to lunch without me because I didn't have any money, even though I'd spent a lot of my money on her lunch the week prior. A few weeks later, a similar event happened with another friend of mine, and the results were different. This particular friend had come to my department and we started talking about any and everything we could think about. We talked so much that we lost track of time. And I didn't normally go to lunch with her because we worked in different departments, plus, she didn't have a steady schedule like me. Nevertheless, she'd been scheduled to work the same hours I worked that particular week. When I realized it was lunch time, I asked her if she wanted to go to lunch. She told me that she didn't have any lunch money and she'd catch me when I got back. "No, I got you," I said, insisting that she let me take her out. This happened everyday that week. I kept taking her out, and I could tell that she didn't feel comfortable having me repeatedly pay for her food, but I wouldn't take no for an answer. The next week, I was broke. All the same, she'd been scheduled to work the same hours that I worked that week. She'd come to work that Monday morning, and she was excited about some money she'd received. I don't remember where it came from; I think it was back child support, but I can't say for sure. When lunch time came around, she walked over to my department and asked if I was ready for lunch. I told her that I didn't have any money. I'll never forget her response. She said, "Girl, you'd better come on here! You took me out to eat last week; I got you this week!" In the first friendship dynamic, it is clear that she wasn't my friend because when it was her time to lower herself and lift me up, she got off the seesaw. One of the greatest tests of friendship is need. If the other person does not balance out the friendship by giving as much as he or she is taking, that person isn't a friend. Now, I don't mean that the relationship will be balanced. In most friendship dynamics, there is a slight imbalance, but you'll notice that both parties involved are doing their best to help one another out. In the other friendship dynamic, she was my friend; she'd taken from me, and when it was time for her to lift me up, she did just that. She watched me eat my food and my pride for five days straight. The same is true in marital relationships. Occasionally, the wife has to take on the headship position if her husband is incapacitated in any way. For example, if he loses his job, she has to pay the bills. If he's hurt, the wife has to take on the roles and responsibilities that her husband ordinarily upheld. And again, she has to be a help meet even when her husband is employed, healthy and sane. Every good relationship moves; this means that it shifts up and down, with every party involved doing their part to keep that relationship alive. This up and down movement is the life of the relationship; it keeps the relationship alive and thriving. In non-tiered relationships, you will almost always find competition and offense lurking in the shadows.

How do you balance out a friendship? Try to out-give your friends or, at minimum, give as much as you take. Also, consider how you rank next to each friend. What this means is—if your friend is more spiritually, mentally and emotionally mature than you are, chances are, you are the Consumer in that relationship. This means that you take quite a bit. What are you doing to balance it out? In this particular dynamic, it is common to hear Consumers say things like, "Well, my friend knows my situation, and when I'm in a better place, I'll be able to help her out as well." Understand this—Consumers will always defend their positions because they are receiving the benefits of that relationship, but a true friend will find a way to be a blessing in return. It doesn't have to be a monetary blessing; it can be something as simple as helping your friend in one of their areas of need (weight loss, organizing their home, babysitting their children, etc.). So, if someone tells you about their situation in an attempt to defend their position in your life, ask yourself these questions:

1. **How long has the individual in question been in that position?** If the person has been in that state for years, chances are, he or she will never come out of it, or you may be hindering that person's growth by pacifying the individual's entitlement.

2. **Does the individual in question balance out the other relationships that he or she is a part of?** You'll find that Consumers tend to give to other Consumers, but they often feel entitled to the resources of their Producer friends. This is because they reason this way, "It's not like she doesn't have it" or "He can afford to give; he has more than enough!" Howbeit, you will find them on social media posting pictures of dinner dates with their other Consumer friends, and they'll make it known that they've paid for the dinner, even though you have to pay most of the time whenever they invite you out to eat.

3. **Do I hear or see this person whenever the individual's needs are met?** You'll find that Consumers tend to call less frequently whenever they have an abundance of money or whenever they find themselves in a new relationship with someone

who appears (to them) to be promising.

When a friendship is chronically imbalanced, we see the "strong friend" dynamic beginning to surface. In truth, most Producers serve as the "strong friends" in the majority of their peer and familial relationships. This is why Producers often go into isolation. Over the course of time, they begin to feel taken advantage of. The person on the receiving end (Consumer) is usually very happy with the relationship. If the Producer complains about the dynamic, the Consumer may say something to the effect of, "I don't know what the problem is. I have no complaints about you or our friendship. I think you're amazing! I pray for you all the time!" This is because it is possible to be a friend to someone who, in return, is not your friend. The beneficiary or the one receiving the friendship benefits will want things to remain just as they are, but the Producer will often wrestle with whether or not he or she should cut all ties with the other person. In the strong friend/beneficiary dynamic, the strong friend adapts to being the giver, whereas the Consumer adapts to being the receiver. This complex, one-sided relationship can last for years (decades even); that is until the Producer grows weary and begins to set and enforce a new set of boundaries. The problem here is that the strong friend has allowed himself or herself to be repeatedly taken advantage of, so much so that the individual doesn't realize when he or she is being used anymore. All the same, the beneficiary doesn't realize that he or she is taking advantage of another human being. After a while, this not only becomes the dynamic of the strong friend/beneficiary's relationship, it becomes a stronghold or pattern. What I mean by this is—the strong friend will habitually create the strong friend/beneficiary dynamic in every relationship that he or she hosts because the individual will grow accustomed to being the head or leader of every relationship. What this means is that this behavior becomes almost instinctual. This imbalance often sets the stage for a host of mental and emotional issues on the Producer's part. The reason for this is because the strong friend often has nowhere to turn and no one to turn to when he or she needs a shoulder to cry on; this causes the strong friend (Producer) to either internalize his or her problems or share them with people who are either too immature or too self-centered (sometimes both) to give the Producer anything other than a listening ear. This is why understanding both your role and your rank in a relationship is important. It keeps you from falling into the trap of being taken advantage of by people who ordinarily would have been great additions to your life had they been given the proper labels and placed in the right circles. This means that you can host relationships with people who don't have as much to offer you as you have to offer them, but those relationships are rarely intimate—at least, on your part. It is possible to host a relationship with someone where the dynamic is, you've placed that person in your intellectual circle, while that person has placed you in his or her intimate circle. But in this particular dynamic, it is imperative that you set boundaries. The reason for this is we instinctively feel the need to open our hearts to people who open their hearts to us. Think of it this way—would you give the pin number of your bank account to a dear friend of yours if she gave you the pin number to her bank account? What if you had $750,000 in your account, but all she had in her account was $30? You wouldn't do this because your friend is not necessarily putting herself at risk by giving you her pin, after all, she doesn't have much to lose. This doesn't mean that she is bad or beneath you; it simply means that there are two extremes present. One person has a lot to lose; the other has a lot to gain. Think of your heart as your bank account, spiritually speaking. This is where Heaven deposits your blessings in the form of talents. Let's look at one of the parables that Jesus told.

- **Matthew 25:14-30:** For the kingdom of heaven is as a man traveling into a far country, who called his own servants, and delivered unto them his goods. And unto one he gave five talents, to another two, and to another one; to every man according to his several ability; and straightway took his journey. Then he that had received the five talents went and traded with the same, and made them other five talents. And likewise he that had received two, he also gained other two. But he that had received one went and digged in the earth, and hid his lord's money. After a long time the lord of those servants cometh, and reckoneth with them. And so he that had received five talents came and brought other five talents, saying, Lord, thou deliveredst unto me five talents: behold, I have gained beside them five talents more. His lord said unto him, Well done, thou good and faithful servant: thou hast been faithful over a few things, I will make thee ruler over many things: enter thou into the joy of thy lord. He also that had received two talents came and said, Lord, thou deliveredst unto me two talents: behold, I have gained two other talents beside them. His lord said unto him, Well done, good and faithful servant; thou hast been faithful over a few things, I will make thee ruler over many things: enter thou into the joy of thy lord. Then he which had received the one talent came and said, Lord, I knew thee that thou art an hard man, reaping where thou hast not sown, and gathering where thou hast not strawed: And I was afraid, and went and hid thy talent in the earth: lo, there thou hast that is thine. His lord answered and said unto him, Thou wicked and slothful servant, thou knewest that I reap where I sowed not, and gather where I have not strawed: Thou oughtest therefore to have put my money to the exchangers, and then at my coming I should have received mine own with usury. Take therefore the talent from him, and give it unto him which hath ten talents. For unto every one that hath shall be given, and he shall have abundance: but from him that hath not shall be taken away even that which he hath. And cast ye the unprofitable servant into outer darkness: there shall be weeping and gnashing of teeth.

In this parable, we see the following:

Unfaithful Servant	Faithful Servant x 2	Faithful Servant x 5
1 Talent	2 Talents	5 Talents

Of course, the unfaithful servant buried his talent, and when his master returned, he took even that one talent away from him because of his distrust/lack of faith. Of course, a lack of faith leads to disloyalty or unfaithfulness. For example's sake, let's imagine that the middle guy (faithful servant x 2) had once had one talent, and he'd pushed through poverty, fear, rejection and everything that stood in his way; this is how he ended up with two talents. But before he'd come out of poverty into the middle-class of purpose, he'd been close friends with the unfaithful servant. Because of his understanding of loyalty, he'd decided that he'd never abandon any of his friends. And while this is great and admirable, it is normal to outgrow a friendship, and when this happens, you don't necessarily have to end the friendship. You simply have to keep growing and changing, and if your friend doesn't grow with you, that individual will fall away; that is if you don't revisit your old mindset every time you talk with that friend. In other words, speak the language that your friends speak, but get rid of any toxic mindsets and ways that may have linked you to that dimension. In short, what was once a relative (eye-to-eye) relationship may transform into a different type of relationship; she may become your baby sister in Christ or he may become someone you're mentoring. You don't necessarily have to call it a mentorship; you just have to identify your new role with that person, otherwise, the relationship may end with both of you walking away offended and hurt. This is because your friend will keep trying to reach the version of you that he or she can relate to, meaning, your friend will repeatedly try to resuscitate the version of you that you've killed, and believe it or not, he or she may be successful if you don't set the proper boundaries. Going back to the example of the unfaithful servant versus the faithful servants, let's say that Theodore is the unfaithful servant, while his two friends Bernie and Jamal are the faithful servants. Bernie is the servant who had two talents, but before he'd elevated to that level, he had once been close friends with Theodore. And when he had two talents, he was closer on the spectrum to Theodore than he was to Jamal, meaning he could relate more to Theodore. This also meant that he would likely empathize more with Theodore than he did with Bernie. Get this—after Bernie elevated, he likely felt a shift or a difference in his relationship with Theodore. Nevertheless, he's likely been taught what many of us were taught; that is—he's grown to believe that he has to prove himself to his last level, and by this, I mean he's come to believe that he has to work extra hard to prove to Theodore that he's still the same man who once had one talent, not realizing that he doesn't have to end his relationship with Theodore. He just has to respect the level he's on. This feat isn't easy because Bernie may say to himself, "If Jamal and I started hanging out, I could let go of Theodore, after all, I know that Theodore isn't my friend." Howbeit, Jamal would have more to lose if he were to form a friendship with Bernie. He could mentor Bernie, but allowing Bernie into his intimate circle could ultimately slow down Jamal's progress. You see, Jamal has committed more time to developing and expressing his gifting, whereas Bernie is producing at a different speed limit. So, if Jamal formed a friendship with Bernie, there's a high probability that Bernie would want to spend quite a bit of time talking on the phone with Jamal or hanging out, and again, this would slow Jamal down. I'm saying that to say this—a relationship between the two men would have to be tiered. Bernie wants to befriend Jamal, but Jamal is loyal to his purpose. The best solution to this is for Bernie to ask Jamal to be his mentor. Can a friendship form between the two? Yes, over the course of time when Bernie matures enough to understand how to navigate the realm of honor. For example, I have friends who, spiritually speaking, are more mature and experienced than me; some of them outrank me spiritually. So, for the most part, they serve as mentors in my life. However, we have friendship moments. Most of the time when we speak over the phone, we're navigating the realm of friendship. However, whenever they start dropping wisdom, I then switch to mentee mode. This is because I recognize that our relationship is tiered. And by mentee mode, I mean that I listen and take notes. I also ask questions. Additionally, I don't ever call them by their names; I refer to them by their titles (if they have any). I also refer to them as "sir" or "ma'am." And right there in the middle of a mentorship moment, they'll suddenly switch back to friend mode. Consider the complex relationship that Abram (later known as Abraham) had with his nephew, Lott. Let's look at some scriptures:

- **Genesis 12:1-3:** Now the LORD had said unto Abram, Get thee out of thy country, and from thy kindred, and from thy father's house, unto a land that I will shew thee: And I will make of thee a great nation, and I will bless thee, and make thy name great; and thou shalt be a blessing: And I will bless them that bless thee, and curse him that curseth thee: and in thee shall all families of the earth be blessed.

- **Genesis 13:2-9:** And Abram was very rich in cattle, in silver, and in gold. And he went on his journeys from the south even to Bethel, unto the place where his tent had been at the beginning, between Bethel and Hai; unto the place of the altar, which he had made there at the first: and there Abram called on the name of the LORD. And Lot also, which went with Abram, had flocks, and herds, and tents. And the land was not able to bear them, that they might dwell together: for their substance was great, so that they could not dwell together. And there was a strife between the herdmen of Abram's cattle and the herdmen of Lot's cattle: and the Canaanite and the Perizzite dwelled then in the land. And Abram said unto Lot, Let there be no strife, I pray thee, between me and thee, and between my herdmen and thy herdmen; for we be brethren. Is not the whole land before thee? separate thyself, I pray thee, from me: if thou wilt take the left hand, then I will go to the right; or if thou depart to the right hand, then I will go to the left.

Notice here that:
1. God told Abram to leave his family behind. The assignment was given to Abram.
2. Abram took Lott along with him or he may have simply allowed Lott to follow him.
3. Since this was Abram's assignment, this should have been a tiered relationship with Abram being the head and Lott, along with his herdsmen, serving as members or helping hands. Read this carefully: anyone who tags along with you while you are operating in your assignment will either serve as a helper or a distraction! This is why it is frustrating to most leaders when people who are not volunteering in any capacity start whining and complaining about not spending time with them. They want to spend time talking, while the leader is wired to build.
4. Lott's herdsmen and Abram's herdsmen ended up having some type of dispute. The Bible doesn't tell

us what they were fighting about, but it's likely that because Lott had become so rich with cattle, they were likely arguing about what belonged to who. Either way, their riches had been the result of them walking with Abram. This is to say that people can be blessed from walking with you, but if they don't have a relationship with God, they will start to challenge your authority. Abram was wise enough to separate himself from Lott.

5. The story ends with Lott choosing Sodom and Gomorrah because of how it looked, while Abram chose to walk by faith and not by sight. Lott was eventually taken into captivity when Sodom and Gomorrah was attacked, and Abram had to rescue him. Later on, Abram interceded on behalf of Lott, along with Sodom and Gomorrah when God decided to destroy the cities because of their wickedness. Because of Abram's prayers, Lott and his family were rescued (aside from his wife who'd disobeyed God and looked back, thus becoming a pillar of salt).

Amazingly enough, most of Israel's greatest enemies came from Lott's lineage. This is to say that all too often, our greatest enemies tend to come, not just from our family units, but from the people we once walked closely with.

How would you have behaved if you were Lott? In truth, it would have been wise for Lott to simply speak with his herdsmen, but when a tiered relationship is brought to eye-level, the benefactor will see himself or herself as the Producer's equal (in rank). Consequently, the benefactor will almost always lose the benefits of that relationship.

How do you have a tiered relationship with someone you outrank?

1. Never allow that person to become dependent on you for anything; this includes money, affirmation, self-esteem, companionship, etc. In other words, never become someone's everything!

2. Never allow that person to turn you into his or her idol. This is not only dangerous, it is also demonic. You'll know that a person is idolizing you when or if the individual constantly flatters you, starts dressing and behaving like you, and feels the need to know your every move.

3. Don't be so readily available all the time. If you're busier than the person in question, it's okay to set time constraints and boundaries. For example, when I found myself in a friendship like this, I allowed her to call me every single day, and I would speak with her for hours on end. This slowed my production down by more than 50 percent! I had to learn to only talk on the phone when we had something that needed to be discussed, and not waste time talking about silly things.

4. Point them to a therapist when they need one. Help your friends out; don't get me wrong, but know your limitations. Sometimes, people need more than

what you're offering, and by counseling them, you are creating a dependency between them and yourself. In other words, counsel the people in your life, but also put time constraints on this, meaning if they need to talk about an issue for more than three days, suggest that they get a therapist. I even booked a few sessions for one of my sisters in Christ when she needed it. Why is this? I recognized that because of her familiarity with me, she wouldn't listen to half of what I had to say. I'd just be a listening ear. She needed to speak with someone who she was not familiar with ... someone she would not feel comfortable over-talking. In other words, I recognized when she needed a voice other than my own.

5. Never avail yourself to repeated rounds of outward self-talk. What does this mean? Some people don't feel comfortable talking to themselves, so they call other people just so they can hear themselves speak. In other words, they didn't call you to listen; they called you to speak, and while this is okay sometimes, don't allow this to become a constant.

6. Set boundaries and answer whatever questions the individual has. For example, I'd say, "Hey sis, don't call me after ten o'clock unless it is an emergency. Also, don't talk to me about your sex life. Remember, I don't believe in sex outside of marriage. And finally, as a reminder, don't just pop up at my house; call me and make sure I'm not only

available, but I'm open to having visitors."

7. Test the spirit. You do this by getting to know the person and learning that person's habits. A good tree can't bear bad fruit, and a bad tree can't bear good fruit. Howbeit, you need time to see what is repeatedly growing in a person's life. Look at the works of the flesh and the fruits of the spirit. Which ones are prevalent and blossoming in that person's life? This should let you know if that person is healthy enough to have an intimate relationship with you, the person needs to remain in your intellectual circle or if the person should be a part of your life at all.

8. Place healthy speed limits on your relationships. Do NOT let people rush you into an intimate relationship with them ... ever! Take your time and let everything happen organically; this way, you'll have time to test the spirit.

9. Place a time limit on your conversations. I don't mean that you have to do this with every conversation, but with most conversations. There may be times when you have to disregard the time limit, but you don't want to create a habit of spending hours on the phone, especially when the conversation is unfruitful.

10. Don't feel compelled to open up to them just because they opened up to you. The Bible tells us to guard our hearts, but Satan has mastered getting us to open them. One trick that works most of the

time is this—someone will open up to you and tell you something intimate and embarrassing, signifying that the person is extending a measure of trust to you. You then feel compelled and obligated to share something equally as embarrassing. Remember the example about the bank account with $30 versus the one that has $750,000.

11. Don't fall into the strong friend trap. Be a great big sister or brother in Christ, rather than a strong friend who doesn't have any friends.

12. Give the individual a set of solutions, and watch how he or she manages them. This is how you decide whether you're casting your pearls to swine (see Matthew 7:6) or not. For example, let's say that your friend Stephen calls and complains about not having enough to pay his bills from month to month. Rather than listening to him talk about this every payday, recommend a financial advisor to him, but before you do this, send him anywhere between three to ten pointers. If he eats out daily, recommend that he cut that out and make his own meals. If he is always buying name brand clothes, recommend that he start buying clothes that fit his budget. Dave Ramsey popularized these fitting words, "Act your wage." Also, recommend that he start a budget. The next time he starts talking about his financial situation, ask him if he's done any of the things you've suggested. If he says no or if he says that he has, but they weren't working,

don't let him talk to you about his financial woes anymore; it's a waste of your time. Point him to a financial advisor and end the call. Also, let him know that you will no longer discuss money with him.

How do you have a tiered relationship with someone who outranks you?

1. Honor, honor, honor! Never fall into the traps of familiarity and dishonor.

2. Understand your habits; do you respect the people closest to you? If not, don't try to bring the Producer or leader in your life close. Keep them at a distance so that you can continue to benefit from your relationship with them without sabotaging that relationship.

3. Try not to refer to them by their first name; refer to them by their titles or use "ma'am" and "sir." You do this to remind yourself that the individual in question is there to pour into you, and not the other way around.

4. Balance the relationship out (at minimum); don't say "thank you" more than you say "you're welcome." Show your appreciation.

5. Don't allow yourself to be an open door for the enemy to enter into that person's life. One pattern the devil has is—if he wants to get to a person, but that individual is too prayed up and refuses to step outside the will of God, he will use the people closest to that person to get to them. He will look

for the weakest person in that person's intimate circle; don't let that person be you.

6. Don't be prideful; listen more than you speak. Think of a pitcher pouring into a glass. The pitcher has to rise higher than the glass before it can pour. The glass has to remain low to receive. If you insist on being eye-to-eye with the person, you won't be able to receive the wisdom and revelation the person has the ability to pour into you.

7. Remember that the person may be far more busy than you are. Respect the individual's time. Don't call or text every single day.

8. Support whatever the person is promoting (as long as it's good and Godly). Believe it or not, there are people out there who are takers (Consumers) who never show their support to the people they are taking from. This is usually the result of familiarity and entitlement; it's the outward expression of an inward thought that sounds like, "I'm just as smart as her" or "I'm just as anointed as him!"

9. Guard your heart. Cast down evil imaginations that threaten your relationship with that person. And don't forget to test the spirits in the people who attempt to enter your life. Some people will try to connect to you just because of who you're connected to. Don't be an open door for the enemy in that person's life.

10. Don't take everything personally. For example, Producers are oftentimes so busy that they may not

speak to you for months at a time. This doesn't mean that they are no longer talking to you; it simply means that they are busy, and whenever they are not busy, they are resting. Be understanding; show compassion.

Tiered relationships set the stage for promotion. If you want to grow in wisdom and rank, have people in your life who:

- Outrank you.
- Don't rank as high as you.
- Are relative or eye-level to you.

And learn how to identify the people in your life. Lastly, understand that roles do shift or change in the relationship dynamic. For example, someone who was your mentor can become a friend if you grow to his or her height. Someone who is your friend can become your mentor if he or she grows faster than you. Someone who was relative to you in height, spiritually speaking, can outgrow you or suddenly become a dwarf. This is why listening is imperative in every relationship; this is also why you should never allow yourself to become a prisoner of toxic loyalty, whereas you become so dedicated to a person that you forfeit your purpose and your destiny to accompany that person on his or her path to nothingness. Love, honor and cherish every person in your life, but understand that if you want to reach the height of your potential, you have to remain sober-minded and prayerful so that you can recognize

every relational shift that takes place and respond
accordingly.

Breakups and Breakthroughs

Have you ever experienced a traumatic breakup? If you've lived long enough, chances are, you have. If you are still with the love of your life and the individual in question has treated you with honor and respect, you have truly experienced a one-of-a-kind blessing. That's because most people have had to nurse a broken heart at some point in their lives, and truth be told, this is one of the hardest events to overcome. And, of course, we can't limit broken hearts to failed romantic relationships; many of us have had our hearts broken by family members, friends and other believers. In this, we came to understand that there is no true manual that can teach us how to navigate the realm of brokenness outside of a few instructions in the Bible, which includes:

- **Ephesians 4:16:** Be ye angry, and sin not: let not the sun go down upon your wrath.
- **Colossians 3:13:** Forbearing one another, and forgiving one another, if any man have a quarrel against any: even as Christ forgave you, so also do ye.
- **Proverbs 25:21-22:** If thine enemy be hungry, give him bread to eat; and if he be thirsty, give him water to drink: For thou shalt heap coals of fire upon his head, and the LORD shall reward thee.

First and foremost, let's discuss what causes breakups, be they romantic, platonic, familial or professional. There are several catalysts behind breakups; they are:

1. **Wrongful Connections**: Sometimes, we connect to the wrong people because of loneliness, fear, need, peer pressure, brokenness, rejection or because we're attempting to hijack a season that seems to be far out of our reach. In other words, we sometimes connect ourselves to people who are not supposed to walk with us. The breakup comes when our soul admits that we cannot tolerate, endure or host these people in our lives.

2. **Sin**: You can connect to the right people the wrong way, or you can connect to the wrong people the right way; either way, the end result will be the same. Any relationship built on sin is just as stable as its foundation.

3. **Expired Connections**: Let's face it. Some people were never meant to be permanent fixtures in our lives; their purpose and presence in our lives was temporary, and had we acknowledged this, our relationships with those people would have survived the tests of time. I know that sounds hypocritical, but what I've learned is this—you can have a permanent connection with a temporary figure if you connect to that person the right way. This means that Joseph, for example, may have been someone you were supposed to minister to for a few months; you weren't supposed to date him. Had

you prayed about your connection to him, there wouldn't have been a breakup because you would not have connected yourself to him romantically. Your season as a mentor, a coach or a therapist in his life would have ended, but you would have heard from him occasionally (and vice versa) just to say "thank you" or to check in. And while you would no longer have a Circle 2 or Circle 3 connection with him, he would have remained in your intellectual circle.

4. **Out of Season Connections:** Sometimes, we connect to the right people in the wrong seasons. A good example of this is—a woman receives a prophetic word from another woman at her church regarding one of the male members there. "God said that he's your husband," the woman says, pointing to the guy lying face-down on the altar. And while she may have given the young lady an accurate prophetic word, the truth is that the word may be out of season for her, meaning God is dealing with a futuristic connection. Mature prophets and prophetic people know not to give every word that they receive; instead, they act as intercessors, praying those words through until God releases them to release those words. But, in this particular case, let's say that the prophetic vessel was relatively new to the world of prophecy, so she prophesied everything she saw and heard. The woman receiving the prophecy (we'll call her May) is

immature, plus she still wrestles with idolatry, so she immediately begins pursuing the guy (we'll call him August). Neither May nor August is healed or mature enough to host a romantic relationship, but May is desperate; her voids are crying out for gods, and she's not willing to wait on YAHWEH to fill those empty spaces. After a couple of months, August catches the hint and invites May out on a date. Believing him to be her future husband, May rushes the relationship. She kisses him on the first date, love-bombs him on a daily basis and has his name tattooed on her upper back. Feeling pressured and overwhelmed, August decides to end the relationship and run for his life, after all, he hasn't lost it yet (see Matthew 16:25). Consequently, after a year-long romantic fling, an awkward proposal and a whole lot of therapy, the couple breaks up and May is left nursing a broken heart.

5. **Demonic Connections**: The Bible tells us that the weapons will form, but they will not prosper (see Isaiah 54:17). Howbeit, the Bible never said that the weapons wouldn't hurt. This is why God tells us to test the spirit (see 1 John 4:1). Demonic connections are almost always the result of us being immature, idolatrous, impatient or discontent.

6. **Demonic Interference**: The truth is that we need regular bouts of deliverance. I've come across couples who had truly been brought together by God, only for one or both of them to find

themselves in need of deliverance. The problem was that they didn't pursue deliverance fast enough; they got it in the nick of time, but their marriages or relationships had suffered a great deal of damage because they'd waited so long. Matthew 18:20 reads, "For where two or three are gathered together in my name, there am I in the midst of them." Deuteronomy 32:30 reads, "How should one chase a thousand, and two put ten thousand to flight, except their Rock had sold them, and the LORD had shut them up?" In short, there is power in two people who are surrendered to the Lord, and because of this, Satan banks on getting one of the parties involved outside of God's will; this way, the house can be divided. Jesus said to the Pharisees in Matthew 12:25, " "Every kingdom divided against itself is brought to desolation, and every city or house divided against itself will not stand."

7. **Lack of Wise Counsel**: Proverbs 11:14 reads, "Where there is no counsel, the people fall; but in the multitude of counselors there is safety." Pride is the demonic force field behind the lack of wise counsel or our unwillingness to utilize the wise counsel that we have. Sometimes, we trade in our wise counsel for foolish counsel simply because we don't want to do the hard work involved with growing and maturing in the faith. And anything that's subjected to no counsel or foolish counsel will eventually give up its ghost.

8. **Comfort:** One of the greatest enemies of purpose is comfort. This is why we should be consistently building, moving and growing. As I mentioned before, a comfort zone is nothing but a beautifully decorated prison; it's a place that we decorate, fill with familiar things and litter with the graffiti of expired affirmations in our attempts to avoid dying to self, dealing with the learning curves that precede breakthrough and having to be stretched in ways unimaginable.

9. **Looking in the Rear-view Mirror:** I was driving down a curvy two-lane road recently when I found myself looking in the rear-view mirror a few times; this is because I was being tailgated by another vehicle. Normally, I ignore tailgaters, but for whatever reason, I didn't ignore that particular one. We were driving around 35-45 miles per hour, and on a two-lane road, that's pretty fast. Thankfully, I kept my eyes on the road long enough to see a foreign object in the middle of the road ahead. As I approached it, I realized that the object was a basset hound; the dog was alive, well and sitting on the road comfortably. I was coming at the dog pretty fast; all the same, I had a tailgater in my rear, so I began to hunk my horn to either get the dog's attention or to get the tailgater's attention. The dog didn't pay me any attention, and thankfully, there was no oncoming traffic, so I slowed down and drove into the other lane several hundred feet away from

the dog; this way, the tailgater could see the animal in time as well. This worked. We both drove around the dog, sparing its life. I looked in my rear-view mirror again; this time, noticing the cars that were all going around the dog. I inwardly hoped that someone would have the ability to pull off the road and get the dog out of the street. Of course, I uttered a prayer for the dog and continued on (I couldn't stop because my tailgater was unrelenting). Howbeit, looking in the rear-view mirror could have gotten me killed; looking behind me could have gotten that dog killed. What if I had looked up seconds before hitting the dog, and then lost control of my vehicle? This is what happens when we don't forgive people. And I'm not just talking about our romantic partners, I'm talking about our parents, our former teachers, our peers (both present and past), and anyone who's hurt, rejected or disappointed us. Did you know that a breakup that occurred in 1995 with one guy or woman could destroy your marriage in 2022 with a different man or woman? Did you know that every conversation that we have has to be concluded, and anytime we don't get the understanding that we need to move forward, we will continue past conversations with different people? This means that you can easily make the people who are present in your life today pay for the sins of the people who left your life in times' past. In layman's terms, our souls cannot host unforgiveness. All the same, we don't just struggle to forgive individuals; when we give unforgiveness space in our hearts, we essentially become unforgiving; this means that we will become the embodiment of the disease we are carrying in our hearts. This would impact, affect and infect every relationship that we find ourselves a part of.

10. **Anxiousness/Trying to Peer into the Future:** Anxiousness causes anxiety; we only have enough fuel to get through the day that we're currently in. Every morning, God refuels us by giving us a new measure of grace. This is why Lamentations 3:22-23 reads, "It is of the LORD'S mercies that we are not consumed, because his compassions fail not. They are new every morning: great is thy faithfulness." Anxiousness or being in a rush to see, experience or understand the events of the days to come will ALWAYS set the stage for the spirits of witchcraft and control to enter into a relationship, and no person in his or her sound mind wants to be controlled.

Of course, this is a short list of issues that precede or provoke breakups. Another reason that relationships end is because the majority of people on the face of this planet do not understand seasons. Get this—you are not only anointed to grow, but you are scheduled to grow. You don't just go through storms, you grow through storms or, better yet, you grow because of the storms you endure.

Think of it this way—a farmer plants a bunch of seeds on his farm. He's done all of the hard work, but now, he needs a little help from Heaven. He needs it to rain! Sure, he can use the sprinkler system and spray recycled rainwater onto his crops, but there's nothing like a good ole torrential downpour, plus, if it doesn't rain often, a drought would be inevitable. He looks at the skies above him and notices rain clouds. Do you think the farmer will grow depressed whenever he sees darkness ahead or when he smells the familiar scent of rain? Absolutely not! He will put his animals away, secure whatever needs to be secured, and then he'll go inside of his house and wait for the storm to pass. Why am I sharing this? Consider the last prophetic word you've received. Did you know that the prophecy was a seed? Did you know that the warfare that followed the prophecy was likely the storm that came to water that seed? Simply put, change is always on the horizon. Always! This means the friends that you have won't always be the same; that is, unless they're in bondage and they are being spiritually and developmentally delayed by trauma, ignorance and/or demons. Did you now that your romantic interest (spouse or non-spouse) won't remain the same? How about your children? People shift; they grow and, at times, they may even shrink. This means that we can't keep holding the same conversations with the people in our lives; we have to keep growing and shifting and we have to recognize when the people around us are evolving so that we can continue to speak to who they are, not who they were. When we have expired conversations with newly transformed people, we will talk ourselves right out of their lives. And notice that whenever a person's time in your life is coming to an end, that person will repeatedly remind you of the past. This is because the individual in question has no place in your future.

Of course, not all breakups are God-instituted, God-approved or God-ordained. Some of them are demonic, while others are just the products of ignorance, pride and emotional instability. The way to differentiate what's of God, what's of the devil and what's flesh-related is:

1. God-approved relationships were initiated, affirmed and confirmed by God, oftentimes through two or more witnesses. Note: by witnesses, I'm not talking about a drunk aunt, a perverted uncle, a double-minded friend or a fortune cookie. "This is the third time I am coming to you. Every fact is to be confirmed by the testimony of two or three witnesses" (2 Corinthians 13:1).

2. Demonically arranged relationships require a sin offering to continue. Once the sin offering is consumed, another sin offering must be given to sustain the relationship.

3. Flesh-established relationships are centered around temporary carnal needs and desires; these types of relationships are sensual, meaning, they are driven by the five senses. This is why they typically don't last any more than three to five years; that is unless the couples invite drugs, alcohol and/or other

people into their bedroom. It goes without saying that these relationships are demonic, but they aren't often brought together by demonic entities; they are brought together by flesh that has not been crucified.

4. God-approved relationships are oftentimes attacked when the couples involved in them are on the edge of a breakthrough, whereas, demonically driven relationships experience warfare when one or both of the parties involved begins to ascend in the things of God. For example, if Betty starts going to church more, and she surrenders her life and soul to God, her husband, James, may start feeling displaced in her life. This is because James is a void-filler, and the more Betty allows God to heal her life and fill her voids, the less of a hero James becomes. Over time, James will be kicked off the throne in that area of Betty's heart, and God will take His place. Consequently, Betty will sober up and James will have to audition for another role in Betty's life; this means that he will essentially become a widow every time she dies to herself. That is, of course, if the two of them are married. Consequently, James will have to court the new Betty. Please note that this particular event happens in all marriages; people grow and die to the versions of themselves that are no longer needed or relevant. They evolve into better, more mature versions of themselves. This is why we have to familiarize ourselves with change.

All the same, demonically arranged relationships can rarely survive change, especially God-instituted changes.

And understand this:

1. First, there is brokenness. Brokenness emerges when the lies we've come to believe are confronted by the truths we've ignored. Again, this is in all relational types.
2. Personal brokenness is followed by a corporate breakdown; this is when a relationship begins to crumble and fall apart.
3. Breakdowns precede breakups.
4. Breakups precede heartbreaks.
5. And if we heal properly, heartbreaks set the stage for breakthroughs.

Did you know that the average person will go to his or her grave never knowing what it's like to be truly loved by another human being outside of his or her parents and/or immediate family members? Did you know that most people don't know what love is? They've accepted the belief that love is an emotion when, in truth, love cannot be contained in our emotions. God is love, and while there is an emotional component to love, love itself is not a feeling. This is why the Bible tells us that love never fails. Additionally, I've learned that we don't necessarily breakup with people; we breakup with beliefs, politics, doctrines and the like. The people who are a part of our lives are there because they believe much of what we believe, so when we change our minds, we fall out of agreement with them. Remember, two cannot walk together unless they are in agreement (see Amos 3:3) and a house divided against itself cannot stand (see Mark 3:25). In other words, our breakthroughs can set the stage for our breakups. This is why God told us to seek the Kingdom of God and all of His righteousness first (see Matthew 6:33); this way, He would add everything else to us, including the desires of our hearts. All the same, He would add no sorrow to it. God knows that when we connect to people first, we will soul-tie ourselves to people who share in our beliefs, but He also knows that the moment we truly connect to Him, those beliefs will begin to dissipate. Consequently, we will suffer through a bunch of failed relationships. And, get this—a soul tie is comprised of everything that connects the mind, will and emotions of one person to the mind, will and emotions of another human being. Of course, what connects us are:

1. Shared beliefs.
2. Shared goals.
3. Shared plans.

When we decide to walk together, to build together or to fight together, we have entered into a soul tie or, better yet, an agreement. Howbeit, these surface-level plans of ours are established on deep-rooted beliefs, some of which we do not share. For example, let's create two characters: Brad and Margaret. The two meet at the opera after

Brad's daughter almost fell down a flight of steps. Margaret had come to Bella's rescue, throwing her body in front of the six-year old, thus preventing her from falling. And Brad couldn't be more grateful because, while he truly loved his daughter, he was currently in a custody battle with Bella's mother. Just three weekends prior to this event, Bella had jumped out of a swing set at the park while she was spending the weekend with her father. Consequently, she ended up needing stitches. Six months before that particular incident, Bella had burned her hand with her father's iron while spending the weekend with him. Brad had ironed one of his favorite shirts earlier that day, and he'd forgotten to unplug the iron. After he'd fallen asleep on the couch while watching what he'd described as "the most disappointing football game ever," a curious Bella had made her way over to the ironing board and attempted to iron one of her dolls' dresses. This ended badly, as the weight of the iron proved to be too great for Bella. She'd used her left arm to hold the dress down, but while lifting the iron, she'd dropped it. The iron fell onto her arm, and Brad was scared out of his sleep by one of the most piercing sounds he'd ever heard. As you can see, Bella is somewhat adventurous, and her father, Brad, can barely keep up with her.

After preventing Bella from falling down a flight of steps and potentially having to be hospitalized as a result, Brad had hugged Margaret repeatedly, thanking her nonstop while he hugged his daughter. "Don't mention it,"

Margaret said, smiling bashfully at the handsome stranger. "I have a daughter around her age, so I guess my mommy reflexes came in handy. I'm Margaret, by the way." Brad was impressed. "I guess so!" he said, smiling as he extended his right hand. "I'm Brad, and this is my daughter, Isabella, but we call her Bella." After their not-so-formal introduction, the two spoke about a few things from politics to religion, but one conversation brought the two of them together. It was the topic of child custody. "My daughter has to be the clumsiest child on the planet!" Brad laughed. "And that's not helping my custody case at all, because she seems to be clumsiest when she's in my care. Just this year alone, she's jumped out of a swing; she ended up needing seven stitches just above her right eye, she burned herself with an iron that I forgot to turn off. She thought it would be a great idea to iron her doll's dress because, according to her, Priscilla; that's her doll's name by the way, was supposed to be going on a date at eight that night. What does she know about dating? And just last night, she nearly killed the both of us. She was playing tea party, and because she couldn't reach the kitchen sink, she found the next best thing. Wanna guess what that was? Bleach! My daughter found a bottle of cleaner that's 99 percent bleach and poured it into her little dollhouse cups. She then proceeded to bring me my own personal cup of death, and thankfully, the discoloration of her clothes stopped me from meeting Jesus before my time. I asked her, 'Bella, what happened to your shirt?' That's when I noticed the smell of bleach. I snatched the cup from her before she could finish tilting her head back, and by the grace of God, she hadn't drunk any of it yet. So yeah, I'm about two giggles away from a straitjacket." With those words, Brad began to intentionally make a twitching motion with his eyes, provoking Margaret to laugh all the more. "You're hilarious!" she said, playfully pushing his right shoulder. "Yeah, my daughter, Stormi, just turned six yesterday, and believe me, she is effortlessly living up to her name. She's at her father's house this weekend, and he just called me yesterday to tell me that she'd fallen off her bicycle while trying to chase a squirrel. She felt like the little rodent was bullying another squirrel by chasing it, so she managed to pick up a little speed, jump the curb and chase a squirrel until it climbed the nearest tree. But her bike hit a stick and she fell onto the ground face-down. So, according to her dad, she's got a busted lip, a huge knot on her head and she managed to scrape not one, but both of her knees. So, I understand your pain!" With those words, the two laughed so loudly that some of the people in the audience turned around and began to glare at them. After the opera was over, Brad and Margaret continued their conversation in the parking lot. Margaret told Brad that she too had fought her child's father over custody of their daughter, and she'd won full custody; he was granted weekend visitations. Brad also wanted full custody or, at minimum, joint custody. He showed Margaret a bunch of photos of his daughter that he had stored in his phone, and he told her about some of his concerns regarding Bella's mother. "She has a new boyfriend, and the guy makes me really uncomfortable. He has beady eyes, plus, he has three children of his own, and from what I've heard, he doesn't have a relationship with any of his children. And did I mention that none of his children have the same mother? So, yeah, I don't want that guy around my daughter because I don't want her to get attached to him, only for him to drop a seed in her mother and leave." Margaret could barely contain herself. "Oh my goodness!" she shouted, pacing back and forward excitedly. "That was the same issue I had with Stormi's father! We weren't broken up a month before he tried to introduce our daughter to some girl he'd met on the internet! I mean, who does that?!"

After speaking for over an hour in the parking lot, Brad and Margaret decided to call it a night because Bella had fallen asleep in her daddy's arms. The couple exchanged numbers, and three months later, they were talking about marriage. They'd bonded over a shared belief; they believed that while it was okay for their exes to move on, they didn't like the idea of their former lovers introducing their children to their new lovers. This was a crime that warranted a custody battle, according to the both of them. Howbeit, four-years later, Margaret would find herself back in court, but this time, she'd be fighting for custody over her two-year old daughter, Chloe. Chloe's father, Brad, had immediately filed for joint custody after Margaret refused to reconcile with him. So, while they'd bonded over a shared belief, what neither of them realized was that their beliefs had roots. Margaret's choice to fight her ex over her oldest daughter was rooted in the fact that she'd been abused by her stepmother when she was just three-years old. Her father had never protected her, and she was afraid that her ex was moving too fast, thus potentially exposing her daughter to danger. Brad's decision to fight his ex over his oldest daughter had everything to do with his desire to control her. You see, Brad is a narcissist, and a good-looking one at that. Charming, intelligent, successful and athletic, Brad appeared to be the perfect catch, but Brad, according to Margaret, was a dimpled disease that nobody deserved to catch. What's the point here? It's simple. We can soul-tie ourselves to other people on the surface-level, not knowing what lies beneath the surface. This is why we have to pray, be accountable, ask questions and stay within the safety of God's will when we're getting to know someone.

What should you do if you find yourself at the end of a relationship?
1. If the unbeliever wants to depart, let them depart (see 1 Corinthians 7:15).
2. Be angry, but don't sin (see Ephesians 4:26).
3. Seek wise counsel (see Proverbs 12:15).
4. Be intentional, not emotional; do not be led by how you feel. Feel the hurt; that's inevitable, but don't obey it.
5. Pray. This is how you cast your burdens on the Lord

(see Psalm 55:22).

6. Take accountability; you'll heal a lot faster if you do (see James 5:16).

7. Honor your way out. Don't be vengeful. The way to enter a new season is by honoring the old one, even if it's a season you should not have entered.

Relational Retardation

Did you know that there are different types of relationships, and each relational category requires a different diet of experiences, affirmations and attention? If you answered yes, you are a rare gem. Most people weigh all of their relationships on the same scale because relational acuity is somewhat of a foreign concept to the average westerner. Consequently, a large majority of people can only host friendships or relationships in a limited amount of categories. This not only limits their movements in the realm of the spirit, but it also limits their knowledge, empathy and their capacity to love others. The truth is, a lot of believers don't know how to have relationships with people who stand outside of their understanding. What I mean by this is, they keep recycling the same conversations and doing the same things with the same folks, and this leads to pride, stubbornness and an addiction to gossip. In other words, people get stuck in their last seasons simply because they're eating the same diet of words and experiences, and this causes what I call relational obesity in some areas and relational undernourishment in other areas. Please be reminded that we are all multidimensional creatures. There are many sides to all of us, and each one of those sides has to be fed and grown. All the same, we have to fast in those areas from time to time. However, when we only focus on the sides that we know and like or the sides that make us common, we become gluttons in those areas, all the while, starving the parts of us that make us unique. Whatever we don't feed, we starve, thus relinquishing our authority to the enemy in those dimensions. This causes people to get stuck in seasons and cliques. This is typically the product of people surrounding themselves with folks who tell them what they want to hear or what they don't mind hearing on repeat. All the same, it is also rooted in rejection, the fear of rejection and the fear of abandonment. This limits a person's ability to host relationships with people who are not like them, people they don't agree with, people who may not agree with them or people who challenge their views and perspectives. Most people fear entertaining relationships with people who don't necessarily match the plans they have for themselves or the perspectives they have of themselves, and believe it or not, this often causes them to delay what God is doing in their lives. After all, wherever there is no empathy and love, there will be no favor. I think about how I was raised, for example. Because we were poor, we didn't have a lot of food options on our plates. Our daily meals consisted of a starchy side like rice or macaroni and cheese, and we would have a single piece of meat to pair with that side. In other words, the only balanced meals we ate were at school, and even then, we didn't eat everything that was on our trays. Because of this, we would often have way more carbs on our plates than we should have had, and we'd wash it all down with sweet tea, or when we were at school, we'd wash it down with chocolate milk. This eating habit followed me throughout most of my adult years; that was until recently when I came to realize just how unhealthy my diet was. Breaking this habit has not been easy; I'm still learning to silence the noise of those old, toxic patterns. I share this to help you see the correlation between an imbalanced meal and an imbalanced relational diet. And I must admit, I was severely guilty of limiting myself with people. I fell into the "best friend" trap a few times in my life. I'm not saying that there is something wrong with having a close or a best friend. The problem with a lot of best-friendships is that they are typically built on voids and they create a type of relational inflexibility that is mostly seen in gangs. How so? Truth is, as humans, we are terrified of being alone or not having someone in our corner, so when we enter a season, an institution, an organization, a school or any communal space, we feel the pressure to "partner up" with someone so that we won't feel like outcasts, we'll have someone to share our fears, insecurities and plans with, we won't be the targets of bullies and we can receive help whenever we need it. And when we come in contact with someone who can relate to us in one or more areas, we tend to show ourselves extra friendly in hopes that the person will reciprocate. If and when the individual does this, we then start our platonic dating routine with them; the goal here is to get to know them better and let them get to know the sides of us that we favor. And in most of these instances, we've already decided that we want to be best friends with the people we've selected. But how many times have you come across a group of people who consider themselves to be best friends? Only a handful, right? Do you know why this is? It has very little to do with one person being introverted; it has everything to do with relational retardation. What is relational retardation? Consider the definition of the word "retarded." According to Oxford Languages, it means "less advanced in mental, physical, or social development than is usual for one's age." I'm not saying that this is the issue in every best-friendship that is comprised of a few people, I'm saying that a lot of best-friendships are built on the following:

- Fear and insecurity.
- Entitlement.
- A desire to serve as the principalities (principal setters) over a communal space like a school, a job, an organization, etc.
- Common interests, goals and objectives.
- Common enemies and/or grievances.
- Familiar spirits.
- Need (Dependency and co-dependency).
- Jealousy and envy for one another or others.
- Proximity (Survival).
- Trauma.

Of course, this is just a short list of reasons that some best-friendships are established. In some of the best-friendships I've hosted, I've had the unique and very odd pleasure of hearing my friends tell me that they either didn't like me being friends with other people or requesting that I keep my friendships with them separate from my other friendships. I remember a former friend of mine getting upset because I'd called her on three-way to introduce her to another friend of mine. I'd spoken so highly of the women to one another, and I was sure that they'd hit it off well. This didn't happen. After I hung up the phone, my competitive friend called me back to rebuke me about calling her with another one of my friends on the line. I remember her saying something to the effect of, "I know that you have other friends and I respect that, but my time with you is my time with you; her time with you is her time with you." She didn't say those words exactly, but she said something along those lines. I was taken aback because I didn't understand why this had upset her and why she was being so territorial over me. But this hadn't been the first time I'd experienced something like that. I'd witnessed this behavior when I was around 19-years old as well. I'd surprised one of my old friends who'd come into town by driving her over to my best friends' house. After we left, she'd expressed to me that she felt jealous whenever she heard me referring to other people as my friends. While I appreciated her honesty, I can be honest and say that I thought this behavior was weird. Maybe this is because I've never wrestled with competitiveness. For one, I've never understood why people compete with others. It has never made sense to me, and this is likely because I've never witnessed my mother competing with others. I've seen some of my relatives and some of her friends competing with and comparing themselves to her, and I can remember begging her to close the doors on those relationships, but she would always counter my pleas with, "Family's family" or "Yeah, they just got problems." After this, she'd go on hosting those relationships and dealing with the warfare that came with them. Funny enough, that friend who'd told me that she didn't like hearing me talk about my other friends had shown her competitive side when we'd met as children. She'd moved into my neighborhood, and we'd instantly hit it off, but I had another friend in that neighborhood, and that friend happened to be my best friend. I remember my new friend (we'll call her Charlotte) saying to me that she didn't believe my best friend (we'll call her Lena) was actually my friend. She then went on to tell me that she wanted to test her to see if she was trustworthy. At the time, we were around 11 or 12-years old. I agreed to let her test Lena, and that's when she shared her diabolical plan with me. "I'm going to start talking about you the next time I'm alone with her, and if she falls into the trap, I'll let you know." Somehow, I knew that Lena would fail the test. Anyhow, a day or two later, Charlotte knocked on my door. "Can you come outside?" she asked. She was great at giving eye contact; maybe it was because her big brown eyes were as beautiful as they were piercing. Charlotte looked concerned, upset and determined. I slipped some shoes on my feet, and that's when Charlotte started telling me the results of her experiment. Lena had failed the test with flying colors. The moment Charlotte mentioned my name, Lena was more than anxious to tell her what she felt about me. I've never forgotten her words. Charlotte said, "She told me that you think you're all that." After this, she went on to tell me stories that only Lena knew. I was angry; I felt betrayed, but I also felt grateful. In front of me was this young lady who seemed to care about me, even though she barely knew me. "That's why I never liked her," Charlotte said. "I could tell that she wasn't your friend." After that, I confronted Lena, briefly ended my friendship with her, and shortly after that, Charlotte became my closest friend. Lena and I eventually reconciled as friends, after all, we'd argued, fought and had our fair share of disagreements, so a little gossip wasn't strong enough to end our friendship, but we didn't speak for a month or two after that incident outside of a few driveway shouting matches. I remained friends with both ladies all the up into my twenties and eventually, we just all went our separate ways. We never became enemies. As a matter of fact, Lena and I remained connected on social media and we occasionally engage each other's statuses, but we have not spoken in over a decade.

Why was Charlotte uncomfortable with me having friends other than herself? The truth of the matter is, some people are afraid of sharing their friends with other people, especially the people they consider to be their best friends. The reason for this is they fear abandonment. All the same, they see a quality in their friends that they believe to be invaluable. In other words, they wrestle with comparison and competition. They are hunted with thoughts like,

- What if she likes her more than she likes me?
- What if they talk about me?
- What if my best friend shares my secrets with her other friends?
- What if she discovers that I'm not good enough for her or she starts to believe that she's too good for me?

Then again, social isolation is also one of the hallmarks of a narcissist. I'm in no way saying that Charlotte was a narcissist. I truly don't know if she was or was not. We lost touch in our early twenties, and even before then, we weren't that close, but people with Narcissistic Personality Disorder and people who fall on the narcissistic spectrum not only wrestle with jealousy, but they can and will isolate you from any and everyone who cares about you. They do this by:

1. Communicating their disdain or dislike for someone in your life.
2. Claiming to be disliked or even mismanaged by someone in your life.
3. Dominating your time; this way, you don't have time for anyone other than them.
4. Using gossip and/or slander to sever the ties between you and anyone they feel poses as a threat to their agendas.
5. Sabotaging, harming or threatening the people in your life that they want gone.
6. Move you away from the people who pose as a

threat to them (that's if you're married to them).

7. Attempt to get you or the people they view as threats terminated from your job if that person is one of your co-workers.

This is just a short list of the evils that a person with Narcissistic Personality Disorder or someone on the narcissistic spectrum would do in order to isolate you. This is to say that you should always look for other signs of NPD if one of the people in your life expresses his or her disdain for you having friends outside of himself or herself, or if the individual attempts to sabotage those relationships in any way. All the same, people who are limited in their abilities to host relationships with other people will also show signs of territorial behavior. Again, this is rooted in fear of abandonment; it is also a form of objectification, which is a narcissistic trait. Understand this—every human being has traces of narcissism, after all, narcissism centers itself around selfishness, self-preservation, self pity and selfish gain. Simply put, in its earliest stages, narcissism is nothing but a form of immaturity, but when a person reaches a certain age, one of the signs that the individual is developing at a normal or an accelerated rate is when the person becomes more and more empathetic. If empathy never arrives to replace selfishness, the individual is then considered to be relatively narcissistic. Howbeit, where he or she lands on the narcissistic spectrum largely depends on whether the individual has other symptoms and traits that would indicate that the individual in question truly has a disorder. This is to say that selfishness, including territorial behaviors, can and do fall on the narcissistic spectrum, however, it does not mean that someone who tries to lord himself or herself over you relationally has NPD or any disorder, for that matter. The individual can be immature; then again, the person may be relationally underdeveloped (relational retardation), and just like children don't like to share their toys, they don't like to share their friends.

Relational immaturity is very similar to relational retardation, but the difference between the two is this—a person who is immature in the area of relationships is typically open to meeting new people or learning something new, especially if someone helps them to understand why hosting different types of relationships is important. They will be friendly, albeit nervous, and they will do their best to make good first impressions. Someone who is underdeveloped relationally will strongly object to meeting new people, and if they do find themselves in a room with people they can't relate to, they will oftentimes humiliate and antagonize those people, or they'll choose to ignore them altogether. For example, I had been married for about two years when I'd gotten hired at a car dealership, along with the man I was married to (let's call him Jason). Jason started building a friendship with one of the managers at the dealership who happened to be White (we'll call him Grant). One day, Jason and Grant were in the office talking about the game of Spades, and you know how guys are when they're discussing something they feel they're good at. They can be loud and flamboyant. So, Jason challenged Grant to a game of Spades, and Grant happily accepted. The plan was for Grant to come to our house that Saturday. I would cook while the guys measured their egos up against one another's. They wanted to have four players, so Jason decided to invite his friend (we'll call him Cory) and Cory's wife (we'll call her Samantha). I was incredibly opposed to this because Cory was ignorant, for lack of a better word. He had never truly left Mississippi or gone too far outside of the hoods he so proudly terrorized with his penis, so he was definitely underdeveloped in the area of relationships. When Saturday finally came, Grant arrived at our house first. We invited him in and I made my way back to the kitchen because I wasn't a skilled Spades' player and I didn't want the backlash that came from attempting to use my beginner's skills in a game of egos. The men sat down and started joking around about how skilled they were, and all was going well. That was until Cory and Samantha arrived. When Cory walked into the living room, his countenance changed. "Wow, if I had known that we'd be playing ... never mind." It was obvious what Cory wanted to say. Unbeknownst to us, Cory was not only ignorant, he was racist and I was annoyed. I looked over at Jason to give him the "I told you so" look before retreating to the kitchen once again. Once the food was done, I made my way out of the kitchen, only to witness Cory's racist remarks getting worse. Grant kept "trash-talking" meaning he was playfully intimidating the opponents, and this was okay, after all, trash-talk is a rite of passage in the game of Spades. Grant and Jason had been trash-talking one another at the office; it's a playful exchange of words between players, but Cory interrupted him and said, "Just play," as he coldly and cowardly stared at his cards. He then interrupted the silence saying, "Man, I'm doing you a big favor cause ... whew!" The crazy part about this was, both Corey and his wife were unemployed. They were in the market for jobs, and sitting at the same table with them was a man who had the ability to change their lives, but their racism and relational retardation wouldn't allow them to get past the color of Grant's skin. We abruptly ended the game, sent Cory and his wife home and apologized to Grant. We then invited Grant to come out again the following weekend for a more civilized game, and this time, I invited my friend (we'll call her Zuri) and her boyfriend (we'll call him Derrick). Like Cory and Samantha, Zuri and Derrick were also between jobs, but unlike Cory and Samantha, Zuri and Derrick had a degree of relational intelligence. They had a bit of decorum to them, and they weren't racist or rude.

Saturday came around again, and unlike the previous couple, Derrick and Zuri arrived at our house early and they'd brought wine with them. As the men began their playful denigration of one another, Zuri and I escaped to the kitchen. Not long after that, Grant arrived and Zuri went back into the living room to play the game with the guys. I kept cooking, occasionally leaving the kitchen to watch the game. It was a good game; I knew it would be. The men trash-talked one another, we all laughed until sunset and the game went well. After the game was over, Grant asked Derrick where he worked. "Well, we're both between jobs right now," Derrick said, pointing at Zuri. Grant smiled as he laid his cards on the table. "Well, come down to the dealership Monday morning, and I'll see if I can change that." In honesty, that wasn't a part of our plans, but it worked out so very well in the end. Additionally, Grant invited us all to ride on his brand new yacht with him the following weekend. Unfortunately, we all went down to the Mississippi river in Arkansas, but the yacht wouldn't start. I remember Grant being incredibly angry, but we reassured him that all was well. All the same, we enjoyed one another's company that day. Sure enough, Derrick and Zuri were hired at the dealership, and I couldn't stop talking about how rude and ignorant Cory had been and just how much that ignorance had cost him. Over the years, I've shared this story many times to show people just how inflexible and foolish pride is. What am I saying here? Cory and his wife demonstrated a form of relational retardation; they didn't know how to host relationships with people who didn't look like them, nor did they care to learn. Amazingly enough, Jason and I had thrown a pool party at our house a month or two prior to this incident, and he'd invited Cory and his wife. Cory's wife had never truly warmed up to me; I figured it was because she was shy, so I made it up in my mind to help her feel more comfortable with me. I thought I would be able to break the ice with her, but I was wrong! When the couple arrived at the party, they went to the picnic bench at the far end of our backyard and Cory started playing dominoes with Jason. The pool was filled with water, the meat was on the grill, the music was blasting and we were waiting for a few more people to arrive. I walked over to Samantha, smiled, greeted her and asked her if she'd like to get in the pool with me. She didn't look up at me, nor did she bother to smile. "No, thank you," she said. "I'll stay right here with the guys." I wasn't offended. Again, I thought she was just shy, even though I felt the way she'd answered me was somewhat rude. Moments later, one of my friends (we'll call her Elizabeth) arrived. Like me, Elizabeth was jovial and full of life. She introduced herself to Samantha, and once again, Samantha didn't bother to make eye contact or lift her head. She just stretched out her hand and limply gave Elizabeth a quick and obviously unwanted handshake. Elizabeth tried to invite her in the pool, and once again, she declined. That's fine; sometimes, people take time to warm up to other people. We weren't the least bit offended. So, Elizabeth and I went into the house, put on our swimsuits and climbed into the pool. We then started playing with the pool ball, splashing water at each other and just having fun. Later that day, Jason told me that when Elizabeth arrived, Samantha had looked up at her and commented in the driest tone, "Yeah, that looks like the type of person your wife would be friends with." What did she mean by this? Samantha wasn't a girly-girl; she didn't wear makeup, heels, perfume or even style her hair. She wore a ponytail and she was relatively masculine in her behavior. Again, this was fine, but Elizabeth and I were different. We were girly-girls and we were also a little bit tomboyish, but Samantha never knew this because she'd judged us the moment she saw us. Of course, we weren't wearing makeup that day (maybe a little eyeliner and lip gloss), but we were wearing vibrant colors and obviously Samantha had seen me before when I was wearing makeup and heels. I was so taken aback and offended that I asked Jason to not invite her or her husband back to our house. Again, this is a classic example of relational retardation. Elizabeth and I were trying to befriend Samantha and ensure that she had a great time, but for whatever reason, she'd decided that she wanted nothing to do with us based on our appearances. And again, a month or so later, Cory and Samantha sat in our living room disrespecting Grant, one of our guests. Going back to the game of Spades, Derrick and Zuri were more developed relationally, even though Derrick had been raised under the same conditions that Cory and Jason had grown up under. The same was true for myself; we'd all lived in some pretty rough neighborhoods as children, but my mother had a high degree of relational intelligence. She'd never raised us to be racist. She had intimate friendships with people from many races, and because of this, none of my mother's children grew up to be racist, and I applaud her and my father for never teaching us hatred. They taught us about race relations, racism and about the history of the South (including slavery), but neither of my parents ever poisoned us with racist gibberish. Zuri had been raised by parents who also had a high degree of relational intelligence. Elizabeth had been raised by her grandmother, and while I don't remember what her grandmother taught her about race relations, I can truly say that Elizabeth was racially diverse, after all, we'd had the same friend-group in high school. I'm saying this to say that relational retardation (ignorance) is a choice!

I can't say that I am where I want to be as it relates to relational intelligence, but I can say that I've come a long way, given the fact that for nearly thirty years of my life, I hadn't gone too far outside of Mississippi's borders (minus the two times I'd been to Milwaukee and the one time I'd gone to Michigan to visit some some of my family members as a teenager). I began to grow all the more when I started traveling out of the country. I went to Germany 13 times, and every time I went, I would stay there for a few weeks to a few months. The last time I was there, I'd lived there for six months. In that course of time, I met people I could not relate to; this forced me to listen and learn. It also took away the ignorance of assumption. I can be honest and say that I probably embarrassed my fellow Americans on my first couple of visits. I'd displayed a level of relational immaturity that can best be described as ignorance, but eventually, I put my pride away and decided to learn, instead of foolishly exalting my culture over the cultures of others. I met people from all over the world, and this experience truly humbled me. Today, I have sisterhoods with women from just about every continent. It's beautiful, it's refreshing and it's pure love. All the same, I have a strong disdain for ignorance, competitiveness and an unwillingness to learn.

How do you outgrow relational immaturity or how do you break through the barriers of relational retardation?

- **Admit where you are.** If you know that you tend to host relationships with people you can relate to, and you're afraid to venture outside of those relationships, be honest with yourself and others. This is the first step to freedom.
- **List your fears.** What are you afraid of? Chances are, you've never written these down before, therefore, you may be consciously unaware of these fears.
- **Get therapy.** If you find that you're relationally underdeveloped, chances are, you need therapy to help you address the traumas, the fears and the beliefs you have surrounding people who don't have the cultures or familiar spirits you've grown comfortable with.
- **Get books and read articles.** Study the different cultures, both local and abroad.
- **Don't listen to relationally underdeveloped people!** I understand that your cousin may proudly boast that he will NEVER get on an airplane or a ship, shouting, "I'm gonna keep my feet on solid ground" before sucking his teeth and belching, and

while this may be funny, it's not something to brag about. Laugh! Let him have that moment, but don't let his profession of fear become your reality.

- **Fix your poker face.** Learn to control your facial expressions. People from varying cultures interpret facial expressions differently than we do in the western world.

- **Start locally!** Don't get on a plane and try to connect with people out of the country when you don't know how to connect with the locals. Start in your city or town. Go to some places that you wouldn't ordinarily go to. For example, most of my students are African American, and whenever I challenge them to go out on a Father/daughter date with the Lord, I often challenge them to go to the opera since, culturally speaking, the opera has a predominantly White audience and most of my students are Black.

- **Get your passport and leave the country!** Go to another country, and if you can, spend a couple of weeks on foreign territory. This will change the way you see the world entirely!

- **Kick offense to the curb!** How can you host relationships with people who don't look like you or sound like you if you're easily offended? After all, people are naturally curious. I'm not saying that you should dismantle all of your barriers. I am saying that you shouldn't make having a relationship with you difficult.

- **Learn a new language**. In order to do this, you have to immerse yourself in another culture; this helps to grow your love for the people in that particular culture and diversify your experiences.

All relationships aren't the same. You have to learn to navigate each relational category if you want to have and host a series of healthy and productive relationships. And never exalt what you know over what someone else believes, and of course, don't allow someone to exalt their beliefs over yours. Instead, share your thoughts in love and learn to navigate each conversation with a high degree of relational acuity. Get past the fears and discomforts associated with talking to people you can't relate to and don't forget to test the spirits in every person you meet, after all, just like you don't want to entertain demonized people in your country, you shouldn't open doors to demons with accents either. Get to know people, love them and put each person in the proper relational category (intimate or intellectual circle). Don't be in a rush to have a close friend, a best friend or a lover. Let the Lord grow your relational intelligence one lesson at a time. And lastly, don't limit yourself to the amount or types of relationships you can have, and don't allow anyone else to place their limitations on you. You will find that the entirety of humanity is not as evil as you may believe them to be when you reach outside of your norm to embrace new relationships.

DRAMA-FREE KINGDOM LIVING

I'll never forget the moment when I asked God, "Lord, have I made peace an idol?" To be honest with you, I was genuinely thinking that something was wrong with me because the life I was living was foreign to me. I felt an immense amount of peace, and I wasn't willing to compromise that peace for anything or anyone.

- **Psalm 34:14:** Depart from evil, and do good; seek peace, and pursue it.
- **Matthew 10:12-13:** And when ye come into an house, salute it. And if the house be worthy, let your peace come upon it: but if it be not worthy, let your peace return to you.

At that time, I felt like no one could understand the place that I was in because I was almost alone in this world. Of course, I have relatives, but as I mentioned earlier, I don't have relationships with the large majority of them, and most of the ones I do have relationships with are in Circle 5. I have an aunt who's in Circle 1, but like me, she's super busy, so we catch up whenever we can. I considered getting counseling because I thought to myself that there was no way this was normal. How could a person not have an abundance of relationships and still be happy? I'd heard many-a-preacher teach about the importance of relationships and how it was a form of wealth within itself, howbeit, I was poor in that area if you looked at quantity, but I was rich in that area if you looked at quality. I examined my life and made an invaluable discovery. In the past, I'd always been the strong friend; I was always the friend in need of a friend. I've had many long term friendships, with the longest one spanning well over twenty years. Me and my former friends would talk on the phone every single day for hours at a time. Was this taxing to me? Yep! Nevertheless, I believed that this was the sacrifice I had to make in order to maintain my relationships, and truth be told, I wasn't too bothered by it. After all, I'd grown used to it. It was in that moment that I realized I now had true friends, but what amazed me was this fact—we rarely ever talk over the phone because we are all super busy! This may not sound like a breakthrough moment for anyone else, but it was definitely a defining one for me. All of my friends are busy building ministries and businesses. This is what I realized that day about my friends:

- They don't get offended whenever I miss their calls, nor do they put me on punishment. All the same, I'm not obligated to speak on the phone with them everyday.
- They don't get offended or become argumentative whenever we don't agree about something. Instead, we truly reason together, ask one another questions and laugh at our differences.
- Our friendships are balanced! They reciprocate, meaning they say "you're welcome" just as much as they say "thank you."
- They don't try to compete with anyone else in my life.

- They don't compete with me. There is no competition! I could shout this from the mountaintop! They push me towards greatness, and I push them towards greatness!
- We counsel one another. They ask my input, and in many instances, apply it. The same is true on the other end of the spectrum. I ask for input, and I apply a lot of what they share with me.
- There's literally no drama. They're not emotional, manipulative or easily offended.
- I'm not obligated to share their posts, like their statuses or prove myself to be a friend, other than just being just that—a friend. I do support them, however. The point is, they don't make a big deal of it whenever I'm not engaging them heavily on social media.
- They pray for me and with me, and vice versa.

It was in that moment that I realized that I now had friends who stick closer than brothers. Don't get me wrong. I appreciate every friend I've ever had and I honor everything they've done for me, in addition to the time we shared together, so this is in no way a slight against them. I'm just saying that this was a different experience for me, and while my former friends were essential in seasons' past, the friends that I have now are essential for the season I'm currently in. My past friends played an important role in my life when it was our seasons to walk together. They helped me through many storms, stopped me from making some of the craziest mistakes and they shared their hearts and their families with me. So again, I truly honor them, so I don't want to sound as if I'm saying that they weren't true friends. We were all young and immature back then . I don't think any of us understood what it meant to be friends, but what we did understand, we tried to apply. However, today, I'm experiencing a different type of friendship, and what I'm experiencing fits the season I'm in.

"Oh, Lord! Have I made peace an idol?" This was a genuine question from me to God. Is it even possible to idolize peace? Eventually, He impressed upon my heart that it is possible to make an idol out of anything, however,I wanted to know if I'd made peace an idol. Why did I ask such an odd question? Because I found myself laughing at home by myself; the joy of the Lord would (and still does) arrest me in my home and I often feel God's immense love enveloping me. I often have moments of giddiness, and sometimes, the love of God overwhelms me so much that it begins to overflow in my home. In those moments, I want to hug someone, encourage someone or bless someone. God helped me to realize that I am now abiding in the Lord; I am now experiencing the peace of God that surpasses all understanding (see Philippians 4:7) and I am experiencing one of the blessings of the Lord that makes rich; this was the blessing that He adds no sorrow to (see Proverbs 10:22). I've been experiencing that peace, joy and love for several years, but I think in that moment, I realized that what I was experiencing was and is permanent. Somehow, I inwardly believed that what I had been experiencing was a temporary wave that would hit me every now and again before evaporating into nothingness. So, I would embrace those moments, all the while, anticipating what I feared would follow. In truth, I used to think that high moments like that, while good, would be followed by low moments. It was almost as if I'd experienced an overabundance of love, peace and blessings, and in those moments, I had to do what Joseph instructed Pharaoh to do, and that was to store up some of those blessings so that they could sustain me in the dark hours to come. And there was a season of my life when things truly happened that way. The spirit realm almost seemed relatively bipolar; one day, I'd experience extreme joy, laughter and favor, and then, there was the next day. On that fateful day, I would be hammered by bad news, negative encounters with people, clumsiness and depression. I would then think back to the day prior to that one and almost regret that I'd indulged myself in so much joy. For whatever reason, I inwardly wished I'd saved some to carry me over in my darkest hours. And again, eventually, I did start saving some of the good of a great day so that I could indulge it on the next day. For example, if I'd ordered a few things from Amazon, I wouldn't open them until the next day or the next few days. If someone texted me saying to call them back, and I knew that the individual in question had good news, I'd wait until later that day or early the next day. If I'd planned to go out to eat to celebrate a great day, I'd save my plans until the next day. If there was a movie that I wanted to watch, I'd wait it out. In other words, I'd learned to ration out my blessings in an attempt to not experience the overwhelm that comes with a bad day. Nevertheless, there I was experiencing one blessing after the other, with the greatest of them all being insurmountable peace.

Funny enough, I remember the first time in my life when I'd experienced true peace; this had taken place when I finally stepped into the church where I would receive my salvation. One day, I'd gotten past all of my insecurities and approached the altar for prayer. I remember it all too well. There was a lot of people standing on the altar, some to my right and some to my left. I remember watching my pastor pray for people and lay hands on them, and some of them would fall under the power of God. I'd never experienced that, so I often wondered if it was a real thing or if people were just falling to be nice. Would I be required to give a "courtesy fall" as well just so I didn't make my pastor look bad? Those thoughts quickly went out the window the closer he got to me. I noticed that the closer he got, the more I experienced almost unbearable fear. And, without warning, I saw what I can best describe as a glow around him. It was so bright to me that I couldn't look at him anymore. He was two people away from me when the fear I was experiencing began to paralyze me. I thought about going back to my seat; I even thought about running away, but I knew that I needed to stand right there, so I didn't move. I allowed my emotions to be all over the place because I felt like I had no control over them, but as for my body, I kept it right there on the altar. Finally, he stood in front of me, and I tried to give him eye contact, but I kept lowering my eyes because he just seemed to be glowing. He asked me a question; I don't remember what it was, but what I do remember was when he'd laid his hand on my head, my arms started moving and I couldn't control them. I kept trying to make them stop, but they kept moving like I was running, even though my legs weren't moving. He stepped back and then laid his hands on my again, and for whatever reason, I seem to remember him saying, "Loose her!" I don't think he said that because while this was a REMARKABLE church and my pastor was TRULY a man of God, we were of the school of thought that Christians couldn't have demons. Nevertheless, even if he didn't say "Loose her," that's what I heard. And with those words, I hit the floor. What's amazing about that moment is I remember feeling an incredible blanket of peace covering me; it was so beautiful and so tangible that I did not want to get off that floor. In that moment, I didn't care who looked at me, who judged me; I didn't care about anything silly or carnal. I just wanted to abide in that space. But, I eventually had to get up and go home. I didn't know how to sustain that atmosphere, so I enjoyed my moment of peace before the ushers came and peeled me off the floor. Here it is decades later, and I am now living in that atmosphere; this is why I questioned whether or not I'd somehow come to idolize peace, but what God helped me to understand is:

1. I'd done the hard work; I'd prayed, worshiped, and most importantly, obeyed God consistently. I'm perfect, but I am intentional.

2. Repentance was and is a tree that I repeatedly eat from. Again, this isn't to say that I intentionally sinned, and then tried to use repentance and deliverance as a shower between sins, because I didn't. This is to say that I decided to live for Christ, and whenever I came across another part of me that had to be crucified, I took that part of me to the Lord, and gave it up as an offering. And when that

issue got off the altar and followed me around, I would repeatedly take it back to the altar until I dealt it a fatal blow.

3. I'd made some hard sacrifices; I'd let go of the people God told me to let go of, and I James 4:7'ed some people by setting and enforcing boundaries. And I watched as they fled from my life, reminding myself that God said, "When the unbeliever wants to depart, let them depart!"

4. I'd come against and finally overcome generational idolatry; that issue was many generations strong and I'd fed it half of my adult life, so getting rid of it was no walk in the park. It was a true fight, one that I thought I'd never win. However, when I called upon the name of Jesus, He rescued me.

5. I'd learned to present my body as a living sacrifice, holy and acceptable to God, and get this, I stopped thinking I was doing God a favor by doing so. After all, that was my reasonable service! I stopped looking for a reward for obedience; I came to realize that the blessing that follows obedience is peace of mind (sanity), but if I wanted an overflow of blessings, I had to go above and beyond the standard.

6. I finally said "yes" to God regarding the call, appointment and assignment on my life. Funny enough, in the great and amazing year of 2016, God tossed me into the ring with a bunch of demons, and the first deliverance session I ever did (outside of the one I did on myself) was with more than one hundred people on a conference line. It turned into a

mass deliverance with demons crying out and getting cast out. It all started with a woman coming off mute and asking me to pray for her; she said that something would rape her during the night hours. I knew what it was, so before I started praying for her, I asked if any other woman had been experiencing that dilemma. I didn't want to pray for her, and then have a bunch of people asking for individual prayers for the same issue. All the same, I had never cast a demon out of anyone other than myself, so I didn't think it would turn into a deliverance session. I thought I'd pray, the women would say "thank you," and we'd be on our merry ways. After asking this question, the line became incredibly noisy with tons of women coming off mute; they simply said, "Me" or "I have," noting that they'd experienced the same dilemma. I looked up, wondering what God wanted me to do, but He took over. I started praying and binding up that spirit (won't go too much into demonology in this book), and without warning, all I heard was screaming, vomiting, coughing and demons crying out. I didn't have a pastor at that time; this is what made me start actively looking for a covering because I didn't want to be out of line regarding the souls that came to me for prayer and deliverance.

7. I repeatedly said "yes" to God regarding the call on my life. It's one thing to give God permission to use you, but it's another event to give Him permission to repeatedly use you, especially after you realize and experience what it's like to be used by God. You

lose your life; that sounds poetic, but in truth, you lose the ability to live for yourself. You soon learn that you can't turn ministry on and off again; you can't be carnal from Monday to Saturday, and then turn the holiness back on the following Sunday. All the same, demons literally wait for you to be spotted outside the will of God so that they can legally launch an attack against you. This means that you can't be a citizen of sin and a visitor of holiness when it suits you; this is because ministry is not just what you "do," it's who you are, regardless of what you go through. (Note: ministers that go between both kingdoms often lose their minds).

8. I started appreciating peace so much that, regardless of how "interesting" a person is or may be, I have learned to test the spirit(s) in that person, and if the individual is toxic, demonized or just not God's best for me, I send him or her away. I am no longer a slave of loneliness.

9. I stopped apologizing for being "different" and coming against the generational norms that once perverted, divided and destroyed my family, even at the expense of losing most of my familial relationships.

10. I got delivered from toxic loyalty. I no longer try to prove myself to people who I have to prove myself to. What this means is—I've learned that, like me, everyone who peers into my life from the outside or from Circle 5, has the ability to lift up a prayer to the Most High God; they can ask God who I am to them, and most importantly, if I belong to Him (if

that comes under question). If I have to prove myself to them, they clearly don't have an authentic prayer life or an interest in me, therefore, I won't bother trying to get them to see the version of me that God has blinded them to. This doesn't mean that they're bad people; sometimes, it means that they aren't intentional or maybe, they are seasonal fixtures in my life. Either way, I'm no longer trying to play God in anyone's life. Should they test the spirit? Yep! But, some people don't bother doing this because they've already made up their minds about you. Read this carefully: Never place a comma where God has placed a period, and vice versa. All the same, when a person places a period behind you where there should be a comma, that individual is unwittingly letting you know that his or her time in your life ends at that period. Wherever they place that period is their stopping point, not yours!

Living a drama-free life is funny, but the journey to this promised land is filled with wars and warfare, tears, betrayals, confusion, tests and the like. But the key to not falling in your proverbial wilderness can be summed up with one word: INTENTIONALALITY! You don't have the luxury of being emotional or led by your emotions if you want to break those generational curses that have haunted your family for years; you don't have the freedom to be lackadaisical, and unlike many other believers, you shouldn't be silly enough to think that you can flirt with sin while being married to God. Sure, you have to grow up in the Lord, and when you are a babe in Christ, you will find that sin has a stronger grip on your mind than God does, but intentionality will help you to get Satan to unhand you. And, like me, you'll lift up your eyes one day and realize that you are living in peace, even when the world isn't. Will your life be perfect? Will you be warfare resistant? No and no. But being an intentional Christian will help you to extract the revelation from the warfare, thus helping you to turn the tables against the enemy. Lastly, when you live in peace, you will have peace to offer those around you. You won't go from friendship to friendship, church to church, and from one lover to the next looking for peace, because peace will become a part of your DNA. This means that you will take it with you wheresoever you go! In other words, you will have peace, even in the midst of chaos. People can be outside screaming that we are being bombed and the world is coming to an end, but you'll sit there and experience no fear. Instead, you will have taught fear to work for you, meaning you will cause the enemy to fear you.

www.ingramcontent.com/pod-product-compliance
Lightning Source LLC
Chambersburg PA
CBHW072342090426
42741CB00012B/2886